MW01147355

At ninete...
final targe...
pect who...
ers was a handyman and sexual predator named
Albert DeSalvo. Now, forty years later, Casey Sherman,
veteran journalist—and Mary Sullivan's nephew—
challenges DeSalvo's confession, defies the power of
Massachusetts law enforcement, and tells the world
how DeSalvo may have been betrayed by his own
lawyer, the celebrated F. Lee Bailey. Drawing on a
decade's worth of interviews and presenting startling
new DNA evidence, Sherman describes his auda-
cious alliance with DeSalvo's family, tells how he
strove to bring justice to the aunt he never knew—
and reveals who her *real* killer may be . . . a man
very much still at large.

PRAISE FOR
SEARCH FOR THE STRANGLER

"Casey Sherman has written a book, part investigation, part personal memoir, that will shake the long-
held conclusions about who was the real Boston
Strangler. His ten-year hunt for the murderer of his
aunt, the Strangler's last victim, is a moving tribute to
her memory."
—Gerald Posner, author of *Case Closed: Lee Harvey
Oswald and the Assassination of JFK*

more . . .

"Rich in detail . . . compelling . . . chillingly realistic. Exhaustively researched, this is a must-read for true-crime aficionados."
—*Booklist*

"Casey Sherman has written a penetrating, incisive book that manages to avoid the mawkish sentimentality one would expect from such a personal perspective of so mammoth a tragedy. It is also a model of investigative reporting, raising some deeply unsettling questions about the true identity of the Boston Strangler, questions, ultimately, that turned my blood to ice."
—Dennis Lehane, author of *Mystic River* and *Shutter Island*

SEARCH
FOR THE
STRANGLER

MY HUNT FOR BOSTON'S MOST
NOTORIOUS KILLER

CASEY SHERMAN

WARNER BOOKS

NEW YORK   BOSTON

Published in arrangement with Northeastern Press.
Originally published as as *A Rose For Mary.*

Cover art and design by Dale Fiorello

Warner Books

Time Warner Book Group
1271 Avenue of the Americas, New York, NY 10020
Visit our Web site at www.twbookmark.com

Printed in the United States of America

First Paperback Printing by Warner Books: April 2005

10 9 8 7 6 5 4 3 2 1

This book is for
Mom, who gave me strength
Laura, who gave me love
Isabella, who gave me hope

Acknowledgments

I would like to thank my agent, Doe Coover, and her assistant, Frances Kennedy, for their determination to get this book published. I would also like to thank Joe Bergantino for his help on this project. I am grateful to Bob Stone for his suggestions and encouragement. A special thanks also to my editors, Gil Geis and Bill Frohlich, who both helped turn an amateur into an author. Ann Twombly also deserves much of the credit for this book. I would like to thank Sergeant Conrad Prosnewski of the Salem, Massachusetts, Police Department for giving me access to the case files when no other law enforcement agency would. Thanks to retired Boston Strangler Task Force member Jim Mellon; you are my hero. The following people deserve my eternal gratitude for their tireless work in this case: Elaine Whitfield Sharp and Dan Sharp; Professor Jim Starrs of George Washington University; Dr. Michael Baden; Dr. Henry Lee; Major Tim Palmbach of the Connecticut State Police; Dr. George Stephens, Dr. David Foran, and Walter Rowe of George Washington University; Dr. Todd Fenton of Michigan State University; Dr. Bruce Goldberger of the University of Florida; Traci Starrs; and the kind folks at the John Lawrence Funeral Home in Marstons Mills, Massachusetts.

My thanks also go out to Dr. Ames Robey and the late Tom Troy for helping me to understand Albert DeSalvo and to Patricia Delmore and Pam Parker for sharing their painful stories for the first time. I am grateful to Rick Davis of Van Ness Films for his wealth of knowledge about the film *The Boston Strangler.* Thanks to Jim Collins of East Coast Investigative Services for helping me when the trail ran cold. Dan Rea and Victor Garo offered their keen insight into the Boston underworld and Walpole State Prison. My deep thanks to my colleagues at WBZ-4 News for their kindness and support. A special thanks to Ron Wilhelmson and Cory Silva of the WBZ Graphics Department. To my brother, Todd, I strive to be the writer and—more important—the father that you are. To Jim Sherman, thanks for everything. A special thanks to my legion of supporters, all of whom it would be impossible to name here; however, some deserve special attention: Ken Dodd, Ann and John Russell, Frank and Denise Judge, Cindy Langlois, Corly Cunningham-Quirk, Joanne Griffith, Toby Duane, John and Colleen Somers, Nancy Avia, Alan Otis, Ben Derouchie, Trish Murphy, and Marc Lidsky.

Contents

Illustrations

Foreword

The story of the Boston Strangler is one of those larger-than-life cases in a city's history—in this instance a city's macabre side. The murders of eleven single women in and around Boston during a nearly eighteen-month period between the summer of 1962 and early 1964 frightened and obsessed the people of Boston. Most victims had been sexually molested or beaten. Nearly all were strangled by a piece of clothing or a nylon stocking. Boston police, the FBI, and other police agencies hunted for the killer, but all were baffled for months. Prominent figures in state legal and political circles became embroiled in the manhunt, including Edward Brooke, the state attorney general who would go on to be elected the state's first black U.S. senator, and F. Lee Bailey, the defense attorney who would become one of the country's most celebrated and controversial attorneys.

Eventually, a sexual predator, Albert DeSalvo, claimed he was the strangler. Though he was never tried for any of the murders, he was incarcerated for a number of sexual assaults. First with Bailey's help, and then with the help of a special task force Brooke had appointed—which was eager to solve the crimes—DeSalvo was officially sanctioned as the killer. The Boston Strangler was off the street, the case was solved, and the public could rest peacefully once again.

But like so many big events, it turns out that the

Boston Strangler case was not as it seemed. Movies, television specials, and a number of books have been produced either advancing or debunking the idea that the Chelsea-born DeSalvo was the one responsible for the brutal killings.

Now comes Casey Sherman with his compelling contribution, *Search for the Strangler: My Hunt for Boston's Most Notorious Killer.* Sherman has applied his training as a journalist to review the original murder investigation, tracking down some of the key investigators along the way. Then he turned his sights on advancing the view, increasingly accepted as time goes by, that DeSalvo was a phony.

Sherman has put in years pursuing his mission; he is persistent, indefatigable, and unsparing in his conclusions. In the best tradition of journalism, he challenges power (which, in this context, means the criminal justice system) to build his case that back then the system chose—and today continues to choose—expediency rather than the truth in concluding that DeSalvo was the serial murderer who terrified a city's people and threatened their sense of safety.

But this is also a work from the heart, because Sherman's aunt, his mother's sister Mary Sullivan, was considered the eleventh and final victim of the strangler when she was savagely murdered in her apartment on Charles Street on January 4, 1964. For over four decades the family has never accepted the common assumption that DeSalvo was the killer. Casey Sherman did something about it, even when it took him and his relatives into painful territory. His book is a chronicle of this family effort, a mix of his research and reporting on the case and the impact it had on his family.

Finally, Sherman's work fits right into another important journalistic tradition—that of looking back at a long-accepted version of an event and digging for the deeper truth. He debunks the myths surrounding DeSalvo and the popular version of the Boston Strangler and, in so doing, has made a valuable contribution in correcting a city's understanding of its past. This is no small feat.

DICK LEHR

Jan. 2, 1964

Dear Diane & Family
I have just gotten settled at 44A Charles Street. The two
girls I live with are Pat Delmore and Pam Parker from
Lowell & Malden respectively. They both work at Filenes.
Pat is a salesgirl and Pam works in the office. They both
are great kids. I got a foolish parking ticket today and I'm
very upset by it. I've parked in the tow area about six times
and never got a ticket. Therefore, I'm in debt to the city of
Boston for $5! I am, as of today Jan. 2, employed at the
Boston Safe Deposit and Trust Co. 100 Franklin Street,
just a 15-minute walk. Beautiful building and great people
but figures are not my specialty. It's a very complicated
procedure I'll have to tell you about some time. You may
come up to see me any time, the only thing is that there is
only room for one extra overnight guest so don't bring
your friends, Ha Ha. Say hello to everyone for me. Reply
within five days.

Love, Mary

Diane Sullivan received this letter from her sister
Mary on January 4, 1964, two days after it was written and the same day Mary Sullivan would become the
final victim in the Boston Strangler case. Most people
who read this book have been led to believe that the
Boston Strangler was eventually caught, bringing a close
to one of history's most notorious murder sprees. But
Diane has always believed the real killer escaped justice.

My name is Casey Sherman. I am a trained journalist,
and I have spent more than a decade investigating the
Boston Strangler case. During this time I have seen the
true heart of darkness. It beats inside the killer but also inside those whose job it was to find him. What began as a

murder investigation has evolved into a battle between a victim's family and powerful law enforcement officials in the state of Massachusetts. For not only was Mary Sullivan brutally murdered, she was also used for political and financial gain. With this book, I hope I can finally set the record straight. This book is an offering to a nineteen-year-old girl discarded by the system. It is a rose for Mary, the aunt I never knew.

Prologue : Cape Cod, 1950

The voice came to her again. At night, the way it always did. Mary awoke and wiped her eyes with her small hands, pulled off her wool blanket, and searched in the darkness for her slippers. The voice told her to be very quiet. She must not wake her two sisters sleeping in the same room. The six-year-old parted her auburn curls and tiptoed past her sisters out the bedroom door. The voice was getting louder now. Mary crept slowly by her parents' bedroom door, which they always left open in case the children needed them in the night. "Come outside," the voice beckoned. Mary stepped out into the brisk autumn night. It had begun to rain, and there was a strong wind coming off the Atlantic. Yet Mary did not feel cold as she stood in the backyard in her white cotton pajamas. "Follow me into the woods," the comforting voice urged. The young girl walked forward along the clothesline and toward the row of towering pine trees.

Mary's mother, Florry, was startled awake by a voice outside her window. The clock read 2:00 A.M. "Jack, do you hear anything?" she asked her slumbering husband. Then, not waiting for his response, she got out of bed, put on her housecoat, and walked toward the boys' bedroom. There John and his younger brother, David, were both sleeping soundly. She then opened the door to the girls' room. Peeking inside, she found both Helen and Diane fast asleep, but Mary was gone. Florry ran into the kitchen, where she saw the screen door swinging slightly with the wind. A deep anxiety growing over her, she hugged herself against the cold and ran outside. "Mary . . . Mary!" she called out into the darkness. There was no answer. Suddenly, a flash of Mary's white pajama top appeared along the tree line and then disappeared again. Florry chased after her, screaming Mary's name as loud as she could, but again her daughter did not respond. Finally, entering the woods, she found Mary standing still, the large trees looming over her. "I saw her again, Mommy!" Mary declared, pointing with her finger into the darkness. Florry reached down, scooped up her little girl, and hugged her tightly. Both were soaking wet from the rain. "Who did you see, darling?" Florry asked, alarmed, her eyes darting in every direction, looking for signs of a stranger. "The Blessed Mother," Mary replied.

"She told me to come with her." Florry asked her daughter where the Blessed Mother wanted her to go. "To Heaven," said Mary, not with fear but with a sense of awe in her voice. Florry squeezed the six-year-old as if she were trying to keep an invisible force from taking Mary away. Then she looked the child in the eyes and said, "You mustn't come out here at night, honey." Little Mary was confused but nodded her assent.

This wasn't the first time Florry had gone after her daughter in the darkness. What was pulling Mary outside night after night? Was it her imagination? Or was it something unexplainable? These questions raced through Florry's mind as she led her daughter back inside, tucked the girl into bed, and walked into the small, darkened living room, where she knelt before a large portrait of Jesus hanging over the mantel and began praying for her child. "O heart of Jesus, I trust in Thee, although each joy of life may flee. Though darkness comes, no light is found, and bonds of fear my soul have bound. So when throbs pain or sorrow deep, when heart aweary knows not sleep, my Lord, my Love, I cling to thee. O heart of Jesus, I trust in Thee."

1 : JANUARY 4, 1964

Mary Sullivan could not wait to get a jump on this new day. Even though it was Saturday and she did not have to work, she was up by 7:30 A.M. After a cup of coffee, she'd retrieve her record player and prized Johnny Mathis record collection from her car, which was parked on the street. She had been living in her new apartment for four days now and was getting along wonderfully with the two roommates she once had worked with at Filene's department store. Mary would begin her new job at the bank on Monday, but today she would finish moving her belongings into her new home. Granted, accommodations were cramped. There was only one bedroom, which could fit two beds, and since Mary had been the last one to move in, she had to sleep on the living room couch. But Mary was used to cramped quarters, having grown up with three sisters and two brothers.

Mary's high spirits were not dampened that Saturday by the fact that she was spending it alone. Her roommates, Pat Delmore and Pam Parker, had been called into work at Filene's to help handle the mad rush of holiday returns, but she had promised to have dinner with them that evening. Forecasters predicted the temperature would be in the upper forties: it would be a good day for Mary to explore her new neighborhood. Her apartment was on the top floor of the three-story building at 44A Charles Street in Boston, just down the street from her favorite pub, The Sevens, a small, lively joint with a long bar that seated about twenty-five people comfortably but on a good night often packed close to fifty.

Charles Street was and remains a bustling area. With its antiques shops and small tucked-away cafés, it is one of the few places in the city where Boston Brahmins connect with the lower-income and college crowds. Cutting through the heart of the Beacon Hill neighborhood, Charles Street is just one block from the Boston Common and three blocks from the golden dome of the statehouse. The neighborhood of roughly ten thousand residents is steeped in history. Before the American Revolution, Beacon Hill was a pastureland for cattle. Then builders constructed elegant row houses along the south slope of the hill, which attracted Boston's finest families. The Cabots and the Lodges made their homes here. Then, in the late nineteenth century, European immigrants, sailors, poets, and former slaves flooded the north slope of Beacon Hill, adding a touch of bohemia to the blue-blooded neighborhood.

Mary Sullivan's Charles Street neighborhood, with its cobblestone walks and gas lamps, was the Boston pictured in postcards, not a place where one would expect a gruesome murder. Mary certainly thought it was safe.

That same day, Diane Sullivan received a letter from her sister in the mail. Not waiting until she got inside, she opened the letter right there at the mailbox. Mary wrote that she was enjoying her new life in Boston and invited Diane up to stay. Diane immediately started thinking about the fun they would have in the big city. Of the six Sullivan children, seventeen-year-old Diane and nineteen-year-old Mary were the closest in age and in character, and the two were best friends. Diane raced inside the house and handed the letter to Florry, who looked at the address and sighed. "44A Charles Street! That's dangerous. We're going up to get her as soon as your father comes home," Florry pledged. Diane was confused. Charles Street was considered one of the nicest places to live in Boston. Why was Florry so afraid?

After a frantic day at Filene's, Mary's roommates returned to their Charles Street apartment at approximately 6:00 P.M. The temperature had dipped below freezing, and a light snow had begun to fall. After climbing the long flight of stairs, Pat Delmore pulled her key chain out of the pocket of her wool coat, only to realize that her apartment key was no longer on the chain. Something else disturbed her. It appeared that Mary had forgotten to lock the door. "Mary's gonna have to be more careful. I need to have a chat with her about keeping this door locked," Delmore thought.

She and Pam Parker entered the apartment. The hall light was on, but otherwise the flat was dark. Then the roommates noticed that their bedroom door was open. "I could see Mary lying on the bed in the dark," Pat recalls. "I knew something was wrong."

Parker slowly walked into the bedroom. She could make out Mary's shape, almost in a sitting position near the headboard. "Wake up, Mary, we're home. We're about to put dinner on," Parker said softly. When there was no reply, she called out again. Silence. "I could see Mary's eyes [were] open," Parker recalls. "She was looking right at me. I didn't know why she wasn't responding."

Nothing could have prepared her for what she saw when she flicked on the bedroom light. Mary's breasts were exposed. Three ligatures were wrapped tightly around her neck. A broom handle had been lodged in her vagina. There was also a greeting card sitting on the bed by her left foot. It read, "Happy New Year."

Parker ran out of the bedroom screaming, "I think she's dead. I think she's dead!" Pat Delmore stood in the kitchen, frozen. "Pam grabbed my elbow, and we ran down the stairs. We didn't have a phone, so we had to run across the street to a drugstore," Delmore remembers. "I was so crazed, I spent five minutes looking through the yellow pages for the police department's phone number." Finally she and Parker reached a dispatcher at Boston Police headquarters, who told them to wait outside the apartment building for help to arrive.

Beacon Hill should have been the safest neighborhood in Boston that night. Twelve police officers had been canvassing the area, interviewing residents for a census report. A few moments after Mary's roommates crossed back to their side of Charles Street, motorcycle officer John Vadeboncour pulled up outside their building and ushered Parker back up to the apartment. His words echoed the thoughts of Mary's roommates: "O my God!"

The official autopsy report provided the following information:

The body of the deceased was on one of two twin beds, the one nearer the door leading to the kitchen of the apartment. The body was in a sitting position at the head of the bed, leaning against the headboard. The thighs and knees were flexed, and spread apart. The neck is flexed, the chin resting on the upper chest. The head is leaning toward the right. The body is nude except for the partial cover of the shoulders by a blouse and bra. The breasts are bare. The mouth contains mucoid sticky secretions, a dried strand of this extending from the mouth towards a dried streak of similar material on the skin of the right breast, and on the anterior chest wall. A broom handle is present in the vagina [to the extent of three inches], the whole broom is extending out flat on the bed in front of the body. About the neck are tied three ligatures consisting of (A) a charcoal colored nylon stocking, (B) a pink silk scarf, and (C) a pink and white scarf of floral design. The only clothing present, and this is about the shoulders, is a white bra and a yellow and beige striped blouse. [The first ligature] is extremely tight causing a deeply depressed furrow, completely encircling the neck. [There are] acute traumatic injuries to both breasts.

Investigators also made an unusual discovery in Mary's bathroom. A red plaid ascot had been cut up and stuffed into the toilet.

The oldest of the Sullivan children, twenty-four-year-old Helen, was working as a nurse and living with her new husband in the Boston suburb of Arlington. Authorities called them that night for the grim task of identifying Mary's body. The medical examiner was holding Mary's body in the basement of the mortuary. From the top of the stairs, Helen could see Mary's lifeless body on a table, her feet sticking out from under a white sheet. Helen's knees buckled. She could not bring herself to go downstairs. In her place her husband, Arthur, walked down the basement steps and told the examiner that the dead woman was Mary Sullivan. Meanwhile a large crowd gathered outside 44A Charles Street as detectives marched in and out of the building. The whispers spread. The killer had struck again. One neighbor told police she had seen an older man helping a woman who looked like Mary bring boxes into her apartment building earlier that day, several hours before the murder. Had this witness caught a glimpse of Mary's killer? Another neighbor, living directly across the street, had a clear view into Mary's apartment. At approximately 5:00 P.M., the time investigators believed Mary was killed, the neighbor claimed to have seen a man standing in Mary's bathroom. She said the man had red hair.

One man fitting that description was Pat Delmore's fiancé, a Boston University student named Joseph Preston Moss (not his real name). Moss was among the dozens of people watching detectives rush in and out of 44A Charles Street that night. He had come to take Delmore out for a date. Sharply dressed in a camel hair coat, Moss stood out in the throng of people gathered along the sidewalk outside the apartment. He was talking to Delmore when a cop called him over and took him up to the apartment. Upstairs, Moss told police the roommates had seen someone on the fire escape outside the apartment just two days before. He also said the women were worried about a defective kitchen window. There were no signs of forced entry into Mary's apartment. How had the killer gotten in? Through the window, perhaps? Or had Mary let him in? Was she comfortable with him, comfortable enough to let her guard down?

An aspiring photographer named Joe Butera lived a

few blocks away and followed the police sirens to Charles Street. He was snapping pictures of the scene when he saw Moss, his former classmate, walk out of the building with the police. Noticing Butera, Moss motioned him over. "They . . . They think I did it," Moss whispered.

At around seven o'clock that evening, Florry and Jack Sullivan were relaxing in their living room in Hyannis, Massachusetts. Jack had gotten home late from his new job as a maintenance mechanic at Cape Cod's Otis Air Force Base. He had been working on jeep motors, and he had just finished washing the grease from his sore and callused hands. Because he was exhausted, Florry did not mention her worry over Mary's letter. Then the phone rang. It was not the police, but rather a reporter at the *Boston Globe*. "Mister Sullivan, do you have a daughter named Mary Ellen?" the reporter asked. "No, sir. My daughter's name is Mary Ann," Jack replied, having forgotten she had changed her middle name at confirmation. As Jack listened on the phone, Florry looked into her husband's eyes and sensed something was wrong. She arose from the chair and instinctively grabbed Mary's high school graduation photo from the mantel. "What hospital is she in?" she asked. Jack did not answer. He just shook his head and wept.

Diane says she also had an uneasy feeling that day. "It was a beautiful, unusually warm winter day on Cape Cod, and I remember thinking to myself, why do I feel so sad?" Diane was on a date with Donny Sherman, her future husband. She remembers going to a Yarmouth diner called Bill & Thelma's for a bite to eat around nine o'clock that evening. Bill & Thelma's was a traditional sock hop restaurant where the local teens danced and the music always played. But there was no music playing on this night.

"It was a very surreal experience," Diane recalls. "I walked into the restaurant and felt a hundred eyes on me. My friends and even people I didn't know were staring at us and whispering. I knew something was wrong." Diane and Donny chose a table in the back of the restaurant. Finally a classmate of Diane's got up the courage to come to their table. "You have to go home," the classmate said, her face ashen. When Diane asked her why, the girl would not answer but only repeated, "You just have to go home." Diane says it came to her immediately. "I looked up at Donny and said, 'Oh, no! Mary's been strangled in Boston!'"

On the drive home, images of childhood days with Mary played in Diane's mind. If she lost Mary she would lose not only a sister but also a best friend. All the plans the two had made could be dashed in an instant. Diane did not cry, however. The crying would have to wait until later. Now she had to be strong for Mary. Upon arriving home, Diane rushed into the house and found her parents weeping in their living room. Her father confirmed Diane's premonition that her sister had been murdered. Diane had one burning question: "Where is Nathan?" Nathan Ward was Mary's aimless former boyfriend, whom she had met during the summer of 1961. Ward was on leave from the army after spending three years stationed in Japan. Mary found Ward's swagger irresistible. He studied the martial arts and could break a board with one blow. But behind the macho posturing was an unfocused young man prone to abusive behavior. He had a hair-trigger temper and would often shout obscenities at Mary in public for little things like her hairdo or the color of the sweater she was wearing. Shortly before her move to Boston, she had finally broken off the relationship.

Diane and Mary's brother David, then fifteen years old, was working as an usher at the Hyannis Theater on Main Street, just three blocks from Howard Johnson's. Ward was scheduled to wait tables at the restaurant that night. David pedaled his bicycle from the movie house to the restaurant to tell Nathan the shocking news. Ward was nowhere to be found, however. David would return to Howard Johnson's later that evening, but once again Nathan Ward was not there. This story would disturb investigators, who were told by Ward's boss that he had been working that night. They could not find any witnesses to corroborate the restaurant manager's story.

The next several days were a blur for the Sullivan family. Normally, Mary's parents would have been planning her birthday party on January 11. Now they were planning her funeral. It was a torturous time for Florry Sullivan. She spent hours sitting in her living room, clutching Mary's picture and whispering her daughter's name over and over. Mary had been so young. Why had the Blessed Mother taken her now, and in such a horrendous way? The Sullivan family had been robbed of its favorite daughter. Mary had made everyone laugh and kept a watchful eye out for Diane and her younger siblings, and now she was gone.

Paying for the funeral was also difficult for Mary's parents. Even after cashing in their life insurance policies, the Sullivans were still short on funds, and despite the family's active involvement at St. Francis Xavier Church, the parish did not offer them any assistance. Then the local Protestant minister said he would take care of the funeral arrangements free of charge. This offer infuriated the priests at St. Francis. The monsignor not only changed his mind, but also gave the Sullivans a family burial plot at the church cemetery in nearby Centerville. "A Catholic girl should receive a Catholic burial," he said.

Meanwhile, the murder was attracting global attention. There were calls from newspapers in Ireland asking if the Sullivans still had family in their ancestral homeland. The media had attached themselves to the big story and would not let go even if it meant violating the family's privacy. Diane felt trapped inside her own home by the crowd of reporters camped outside. "That's when I gathered David and Phyllis (the youngest of the Sullivan children) and said, 'Let's go say good-bye to Mary.'" The trio left the house as reporters swarmed around them. "Are you the ones?" a reporter shouted. Mary's siblings did not answer. Instead they held hands and pushed their way past the reporters out into the street.

They walked a quarter mile down the road to Sea Street Beach, Mary's favorite spot. She had loved to look out at the mouth of Lewis Bay and watch the waves crashing against the rugged jetty and the seagulls diving into the ocean for their next meal. On Sea Street Beach, Mary would squish her toes in the warm sand while trying to spot JFK and Jackie sailing off the nearby Kennedy Compound. As Diane held hands with David and Phyllis on that chilly beach, no one spoke. They just stared at the ocean and said good-bye to Mary in their thoughts.

Later that day Diane told the family she would pick out the pallbearers for the service. The group would be made up of Mary's best friends, including Nathan's roommate, Tom Bahr. Diane drove to their apartment to ask Tom to be a pallbearer. While she and Tom were discussing the details, Nathan walked into the living room, screaming. "You can't talk about this here! I don't wanna hear anything about Mary's funeral. . . . I can't take it!" His face was red with anger. Diane restrained an impulse to confront Nathan about her suspicion that he was involved in the murder. "It wasn't the time or the place, so I just left," she recalls. "Besides, I figured if Nathan did it, the police would do their job and arrest him."

Mary's funeral took place on January 11, 1964, on what would have been her twentieth birthday. Florry watched as Diane and David got ready for the service. "I wish we were going to Mary's wedding instead," Florry sighed, her voice cracking. Her thoughts drifted back to that rain-swept night when her young daughter had followed the Virgin Mary into the woods. "She was always searching for peace. I pray to God that she has found it," Florry thought to herself. At the funeral home, Diane walked up to the open casket and looked down at her sister. "Her head was so swollen that the body in the casket did not look like Mary," Diane remembers. "I just said to myself, 'She's not there. She's not there.' That made me feel a little better."

Three hundred people crammed into St. Francis Xavier Church in what was one of the biggest funerals Cape Cod had ever seen. Most of the mourners were family members and Mary's high school classmates. (Mary had been a popular student. The quotation under her picture in their 1962 Barnstable High School yearbook read, "Of more than common friendliness.") One person was noticeably absent from the church that day. Nathan Ward, Mary's boyfriend for nearly three years, did not attend the service. Undercover police officers were sprinkled among the people at Mary's funeral, looking for a suspicious face in the crowd, a face that could belong to the killer. Mourners wept openly as the priest railed against the brutal crime but assured them that Mary was being called to Heaven.

A few weeks after the funeral, someone entered the Sullivan home uninvited. Back then, no one locked doors on quiet Cape Cod. That day, Diane returned home from school, left her books in the hallway, and walked into the living room, where she saw that Mary's photo was no longer on the mantel. Instead, the picture frame had been smashed and was lying on the floor surrounded by shards of glass several feet away from the mantel. Diane looked to see if a window had been left open so that a gust of wind could have knocked the photo off the mantel, but it was the middle of winter, and all the windows were shut tight. The mantel also held several other family photographs; only Mary's was on the floor.

The photo incident was just one of many troubling events that occurred in the months following Mary's funeral. During that time Florry noticed that someone was stealing the flowers mourners had left at Mary's grave. She would replace the flowers, only to find them missing the next day. Then, a few months after the funeral, Diane and her mother made plans to drive to Boston to retrieve Mary's belongings from the Boston Police Department. The Boston Police Department had taken more than two hundred items from Mary's apartment as evidence but promised Florry a swift return of any belongings not deemed necessary to the murder probe. "What about Mary's letters? She kept lots of letters," Florry asked when she arrived at police headquarters. An investigator told her they had not found any of Mary's letters inside the apartment.

On the same trip Florry and Diane visited St. Anthony's Shrine in downtown Boston to present a gift to the priest who had given Mary the last rites. Entering the rectory, they asked to speak with the monsignor. He would know where to find the priest they were looking for. They were kept waiting a long while. Diane had an eerie feeling the priests working in the rectory were going to great lengths to avoid them. No priest came to offer condolences for Mary's highly publicized death.

Finally, the Sullivans were summoned to the monsignor's office. Diane remembers him as a tall, slim older man wearing a long black robe. Sitting behind a mahogany desk, he did not even bother to stand up to meet his guests. Diane and Florry sat down in two wooden chairs across from him, and Florry began to speak. She said, "I have a gift for the priest who blessed my daughter, and we were wondering if you had a lost and found. I believe Mary came here on New Year's Eve, and we think she may have left her letters behind." The priest suddenly rose from his chair and rapped his knuckles on the mahogany desk. He stood over the two women, shouting accusations and questioning the motive behind their visit.

Florry and Diane went numb for a moment. Finally, Diane regained her composure. She stood up and told the priest, "No one is accusing you of anything. We are simply here to drop off a gift and search for my sister's belongings. Why would you say such a thing?" The monsignor deflected the question. "We do not have anything of hers, and I would like it if you left my church," he replied. Florry, who had devoted her life to the Catholic Church, was furious. Mother and daughter stormed out of the rectory and into their car. "I can't believe what just happened," Diane muttered to herself as she stepped on the gas and sped away.

As soon as they returned to their Cape Cod home, Diane got on the phone with the Boston police. She told a detective about the incident at the church and asked what was being done to find Mary's killer. The detective later learned that the priest who had given Mary her last rites had left the church for the Assumption Friary in Woodbridge, New Jersey, where he took a vow of silence.

Silence would be exactly what the family got from the Boston Police Department, too. The phone calls from detectives came less frequently. In the days following Mary's murder, investigators called Mary's parents at least twice a week. But more recently, the Sullivans were lucky if they heard from the police twice a month. And soon after Diane and Florry's trip to Boston, the family was getting no updates at all on the murder investigation. "I remember thinking, 'God, I hope they know what they're doing,'" Diane recalls. Growing desperate, Florry wrote a letter to the psychic Jeane Dixon asking for help. Dixon claimed to have predicted the assassination of President John F. Kennedy. The letter went unanswered.

The weeks and months after Mary's murder were the most difficult of Diane's life. She went back to class at Barnstable High School, where she was a senior, and tried to regain some sort of normalcy. Diane's close friends applauded her strength, but the pain in her heart would not go away. "On those snowy winter nights," she says, "I remember waking up out of a sound sleep and thinking, 'Mary must be so cold, so cold. I even grabbed a blanket out of the linen closet and almost drove to the cemetery before I realized what I was doing."

2 : The Killing Season

The murder of Mary Sullivan struck a particularly emotional chord with the general public. Mary's photo was on the front page of virtually every major newspaper in the nation. Her smiling eyes and auburn hair reminded readers of their own daughters, their own sisters, and the girl next door. Letters from terrified citizens poured into the Boston Police Department and the Massachusetts attorney general's office. The message was clear: Find the Boston Strangler before he strikes again.

But Bostonians did not put their complete faith in the authorities. Frightened women dramatically changed their everyday routines. Some began to vary their route home from work. Others purchased attack dogs. Hardware stores ran out of door locks. Women even began to carry knives. Responding to the intense public pressure, Attorney General Edward Brooke created the Boston Strangler Task Force. The goal of this elite unit made up of Boston and state police was to consolidate evidence from each strangling to separate the serial killer from the copycats. The Boston Strangler Task Force would answer only to Brooke himself.

FEBRUARY 1964

Special officer Jim Mellon of the Boston Police Department rubbed his tired blue eyes and lit a cigarette. He exhaled a small plume of smoke and stared at the ceiling. Mellon was brainstorming. The forty-year-old cop, who had been working on the Boston Strangler case from the beginning, was one of the first investigators chosen for the Boston Strangler Task Force. Mellon kept reviewing Mary Sullivan's case file inside the task force office under the golden dome of the statehouse. The office was filled with bulging filing cabinets containing thousands of documents on the Boston Strangler case. Mary Sullivan's murder was not yet a month old, but because of the media attention, her file was already double the size of any of those concerning the other ten slayings.

Mellon racked his brain to find a common element in Mary Sullivan's murder and the previous killings. Yes, the women all had been strangled, and most of the victims were found with multiple ligatures wrapped tightly around their necks. But the killer or killers of the later victims could have taken this cue from the city's two major newspapers, the *Boston Globe* and the *Record American,* which had recounted the crimes in graphic detail.

If you hated a woman and wanted her dead, you could strangle her and the blame would be pinned on the perpetrator of the earlier killings. Mellon went over this theory in his mind. The detective could not get past the many discrepancies in the crime scenes. The newspapers were calling the murders sex crimes; yet only a few of the women had been raped. The wide range of the victims' ages also troubled Mellon. The psychiatrists he consulted said serial killers selected their victims based on a particular profile. They hunted old women or young women, but usually not both. Thus, Mellon believed these murders were not the act of a single crazed man. But to prove his theory, he would have to go back to the very beginning. The detective closed Mary Sullivan's case file and picked up another manila envelope from the large stack on his desk. The cover read: Anna Slesers.

JUNE 14, 1962

At fifty-six, Anna E. Slesers had witnessed enough horror in her life. She had watched helplessly as loved ones died when Nazi Germany and Soviet Russia fought over her native Latvia in World War II. Anna Slesers did not know how she had managed to survive, and she would never forget those who died for her small country. Vowing that her son and daughter would never be subjected to the same fate, she escaped Eastern Europe with them shortly after the war and immigrated to Boston, which had a small but vibrant Latvian community.

Slesers, an attractive divorcée, found work as a seamstress. By 1962, her children grown, she lived alone in a small apartment at 77 Gainsborough Street, two blocks from Boston's Symphony Hall. Her quiet neighborhood catered to lower income families and college students from nearby Northeastern University.

On the evening of June 14, 1962, Anna Slesers was getting ready for a bath. Later, she was to accompany her son to a memorial service for Latvia's war dead. She had taken off her clothes and wrapped her robe tightly around her small body. Slesers placed a record on the turntable and walked toward her bathroom to turn on the water. As the steam started to rise, the sounds of *Tristan und Isolde* echoed through the apartment. In the next few minutes, Anna Slesers would be dead.

Juris Slesers, Anna's twenty-five-year-old son, told police he had arrived at his mother's apartment just before seven o'clock that night. He knocked on the door of apartment 3-F, but there was no answer. He then returned to the building's foyer and waited for his mother there, believing she might have gone to the store. Several minutes passed. Finally, the son returned to the apartment and forced his way in. The music was still playing. He found the body of his mother lying in the hallway, her bathrobe open, revealing her breasts and stomach. The cord of her robe was wrapped around her neck.

That night, Jim Mellon had been cruising in his squad car on nearby Huntington Avenue, so he was one of the first police officers at the murder scene. He found Juris Slesers sitting on his mother's couch. Looking around the immaculate apartment, Mellon noticed that the drawers of Anna Slesers's bedroom dresser had been pulled out in arithmetic progression. The top drawer was open a quarter inch, the middle drawer was open a half inch, and the bottom drawer was open three-quarters of an inch. But nothing appeared to be missing. Juris Slesers led Mellon over to his mother's body, telling Mellon he believed his mother had committed suicide. According to Juris's theory, she had tried to hang herself from a hook on the bathroom door, but her body had fallen to the floor. There was no panic in his voice as he gave this explanation. "It's as if I were a plumber and he was describing a broken pipe," Mellon recalls now. Maybe he's just in shock, the officer thought at the time. The son had made no attempt to cover his mother's naked body, which Mellon also found odd. Kneeling down closer to the dead woman, he noticed that Slesers's neck was scratched and that blood was trickling out of her vagina. This was no suicide. Anna Slesers had been sexually assaulted.

Phil DiNatale was Mellon's partner. Fellow cops kidded DiNatale about his resemblance to the retired heavyweight champion Rocky Marciano. The likeness worked well when he interrogated suspects. Mellon and his stocky partner went door to door that night, interviewing Slesers's neighbors. No one remembered seeing the woman, though they recalled that a painting crew had been working outside the apartment that day. Mellon hoped that maybe someone on the crew had seen something.

Two days after Slesers's murder, Dana Kuhn, a chemist at the Boston Police Department, called Mellon into his office. An analysis of the fibers vacuumed from the runner in the victim's apartment showed three African American hairs, as well as three canine hairs, most likely from a small terrier. Anna Slesers was not known to have had any black friends, and she did not own a dog.

JUNE 30, 1962

While Mellon and DiNatale were still chasing leads in the Anna Slesers murder, another woman was strangled in Boston. This time, the victim was Nina Nichols, a retired physiotherapist. The sixty-eight-year-old Nichols was discovered on the bedroom floor of her apartment at 1940 Commonwealth Avenue, in the city's Brighton section, just beyond Boston University. Nichols was wearing a pink bathrobe, which was open. Her bra was pushed up above her breasts, and two nylon stockings were tied around her neck. At first, police thought the crime was a burglary that ended in murder because the victim's apartment had been ransacked, with every drawer pulled open, the contents strewn across the floor. On the other hand, a set of sterling silverware, an expensive camera, and the victim's watch had been left untouched. There was also money in the woman's purse. The medical examiner later determined that Nina Nichols had been raped.

The Boston Police Department was now facing an unprecedented situation. Two older women had been strangled and sexually assaulted within two weeks of each other. The newly appointed police commissioner, Edmund McNamara, found himself in a difficult position. Mayor John Collins had appointed him on April 5, 1962, after a gambling scandal had rocked the department. McNamara knew that if he did not solve the murders quickly, he would be in danger of losing his job. To make sure that his department heads knew about the two crimes and their possible connection, he rounded up the police brass on July 2 and went through each detail of the murders. Before the meeting had ended, a detective interrupted the new commissioner and whispered something in his ear.

That day, ten miles north of Boston in the city of Lynn, a third woman had been killed. Mellon was sent to the crime scene, an apartment house at 73 Newell Street, to see if there were similarities between the first two murders and the latest one. The victim, sixty-five-year-old Helen Blake, had not been answering her phone, and neighbors feared she might have suffered a fall inside her apartment. The building custodian was finally called to check on her at approximately 6:00 P.M. Like Nichols's apartment, Blake's had been ransacked. The custodian found her lying on her bed, clad in a pink pajama top. Her killer had wrapped a pair of nylons around her neck, placing one above the other and knotting them separately in the back. The killer had also used a third ligature, a brassiere knotted tightly below Blake's chin. Bloodstains were on both the top and bottom bedsheets. The woman's vagina and anus were lacerated, but the medical examiner found no trace of semen on or inside Blake's body. Investigators later theorized that she had been murdered between eight and ten o'clock in the morning because the autopsy revealed no food in her stomach.

Despite some dissimilarities, Jim Mellon discovered one notable connection between the murders of Anna Slesers and Helen Blake. After noticing a painting scaffold outside Blake's building, Mellon learned that the same painting crew that had worked on Slesers's apartment building the day she was murdered was now painting Blake's. Mellon raced to the MacDaniels Painting Company's office in Boston's Roxbury neighborhood. "What took you so long?" asked Pat MacDaniels, the owner. "It seems women die in every building we work on." MacDaniels, who had had run-ins with the law, was anything but cooperative, but he grudgingly allowed Mellon to look through the company's employee records. But the search was unlikely to be of much use, since MacDaniels paid most of his men under the table.

After talking with MacDaniels, Mellon spoke with the company's two full-time painters, both Caucasian. The men swore they had nothing to do with the murders and said they had not worked with any African Americans on the buildings Slesers and Blake lived in. Mellon sensed they were lying, but proving it would be difficult. The killers had left no fingerprints or traces of paint at any of the crime scenes.

That summer, there would be no reprieve from the terror in Boston. Soon, the newspapers were linking the crimes under the heading "The Silk Stocking Murders," an inaccurate description since only Helen Blake had been strangled with stockings.

Nevertheless, the media and a frightened public now believed there was a serial killer stalking the streets. Single women tried to avoid walking alone. Many kept makeshift weapons by their beds—a pair of scissors, a kitchen knife, or even a ski pole could be used to fend off an attacker. Traveling salesmen saw their business plummet because women would no longer open their doors to strangers. In a 1963 *Life* magazine article, Margery Byers described the effect the case was having not only on women but on men as well. A husband went out to buy groceries after cautioning his wife never to open their apartment door to strangers. Upon his return, he realized he had forgotten his key and rang the doorbell. When the wife let him in, he screamed at her for not first checking his identity.

Some local merchants saw their business grow as fear gripped the city. Locksmiths sold more chains, window locks, and door bolts. Nervous women stood in line outside the animal shelter, trying to adopt a stray. The Boston Police Department set up a twenty-four-hour hot line number, DE8-1212, which was published in every metropolitan newspaper and aired repeatedly on local radio broadcasts. As a result, the switchboard at the Boston Police Department was flooded with calls from women who saw strange men in their buildings or even shadows moving inside their apartments.

Eventually, the police department diverted nearly all of its resources to the strangler case. A new unit consisting of fifty men patrolled the streets by night, all specially trained in the martial arts and quick-draw shooting.

Jim Mellon now was working as many as eighteen hours each day, going home only to sleep. He ate his meals at his desk or while out exploring new leads. The work was grueling for Mellon, who had a wife and six young children at home, but it would be time well spent if he could help get the killer or killers off the streets.

AUGUST 21, 1962

In late summer, police added a fourth name to list of victims. The body of a seventy-five-year-old widow, Ida Irga, was found by her brother, Harry Halpern, inside her apartment at 7 Grove Street in Boston's West End. When two patrolmen reached the fifth floor apartment, they found Irga lying on her back in the middle of the living room floor. She was wearing a brown nightdress, which was torn, completely exposing her body. Instead of a silk stocking, her killer had wrapped a white pillowcase tightly around her neck. Each of Irga's legs was propped up on chairs spread four to five feet apart, and a bed pillow was placed under her buttocks, a display that her killer had apparently set up to mock the investigators. Dried blood covered the victim's head, mouth, and ears, and a blood trail indicated that Irga had been violently attacked in the bedroom, then carried or dragged out into the living area of the four-room flat.

There was no evidence that Irga had been raped. The Suffolk County medical examiner, Dr. Michael Luongo, found no trace of sperm in the elderly woman's vagina or anus. On the basis of a fracture to the woman's hyoid bone, a fragile neck bone that is cracked in most cases of manual strangulation, he also concluded that Ida Irga had been strangled manually before the pillowcase was applied.

AUGUST 30, 1962

Sixty-seven-year-old Jane Sullivan (no relation to Mary) would be the strangler's next victim. Sullivan, who had emigrated from Ireland in 1926, worked as a night-shift nurse at Longwood Hospital. Her body was discovered by her nephew, Dennis Mahoney, inside her tidy apartment at 435 Columbia Road at approximately 4:00 P.M. on August 30, 1962. The heavyset woman had been strangled with two stockings and left facedown in her bathtub. She was still wearing a bathrobe, but her underwear had been pulled down to her knees. Maggots had begun to nest in the moist areas of her badly decomposed body. Police found no sign of a sexual attack. They believed that Jane Sullivan's killer might have attacked her as she was getting into the tub. Nothing had been stolen from the apartment. The victim had been left in this distorted pose seemingly on purpose. Her buttocks were propped up, and her head was partially submerged in six inches of water. Jane Sullivan was five feet, four inches tall and weighed about 170 pounds. The killer must have needed great strength to pull this one off, Jim Mellon thought.

Shortly after Jane Sullivan's murder, task force members attended a special seminar in Boston given by the FBI sex crimes unit. The FBI specialists went over the behavioral patterns of ritualistic killers. Because all the victims in the Boston Strangler case had been older women, psychiatrists believed that the killer had a deep hatred of his mother and might be taking that hatred out on his victims. Soon events would call that theory into question.

DECEMBER 5, 1962

Rain-soaked, Gloria Todd was returning to her apartment at 315 Huntington Avenue after a day of classes at the Carnegie Institute of Medical Technology. Having taken the trolley back from the opposite end of the city in the midst of a terrible storm, she could not wait to kick off her shoes and unwind in a nice hot shower. But when she opened the door to her apartment, Todd gasped in horror.

One of her roommates, a twenty-year-old African American woman named Sophie Clark, was lying dead on the living room floor, a half-slip and nylon stocking intertwined around her neck and a gag stuffed in her mouth. Clark's ripped bra and bloodstained underwear were several feet away. The young woman had been menstruating, and the killer had pulled off her sanitary napkin and left it on the floor. A semen stain was discovered on the rug near her body.

There had likely been a struggle inside the apartment. There was broken glass lying near Clark's feet, a table leg was broken, and an ashtray filled with cigarette butts had been knocked over and its contents strewn on the floor. In addition, the killer had rummaged through some bedroom drawers, and the contents of a purse were spilled on the couch.

There were no signs of forced entry into Sophie Clark's apartment. Clark had seen to the installation of a second lock on the front door, and her two roommates told police that she always questioned anyone who knocked and would never have let a stranger into the apartment. Yet whom would she have let in? She did not lead an active social life in Boston. She had a serious boyfriend back home in Englewood, New Jersey, and had been in the middle of writing him a letter that afternoon. It began with the words "My Dearest Chuck" and ended abruptly two paragraphs down, after she had written, "It's going on about 2:30 now." Investigators believe Clark's letter-writing had been interrupted by her killer.

Clark had been strangled just one block away from the scene of the first murder, that of Anna Slesers. Jim Mellon interviewed all the residents in Clark's building. Three remembered seeing a black man walking toward the victim's front door roughly an hour before her murder. The suspect was well known in the area and also to the police. Discovering that the man had fled to New York City shortly after Clark's murder, Mellon called colleagues in the New York City Police Department, who were able to track the suspect to a friend's house in Brooklyn. That same evening, Mellon drove to New York to confront the man about the murder of Sophie Clark.

He admitted to Mellon that he had been in the apartment building the day Clark was killed, but he claimed he was there to see his girlfriend and that he had left the building when no one answered her front door. The suspect could not provide a name of the girlfriend and no one living in the building knew who he was. His alibi collapsed. When asked why he had fled to New York City, the suspect said he felt Clark's murder showed that Boston was not safe for blacks. Mellon was not buying it. "Hook him up to a lie detector. We'll see if his story holds up," he suggested. Investigators gave the suspect two polygraph tests. He failed both. "This is our guy," Jim Mellon declared.

A forensic psychologist was next to interview the suspect. After only one hour, the psychologist concluded that the suspect was a pathological liar and that his polygraph results were meaningless. Mellon was outraged. "Those headshrinkers always look to put the blame elsewhere," he said. "What they don't realize is that some people are just born bad." But the psychologist's findings were enough for the Boston authorities. Mellon was told by his superiors to look elsewhere for Sophie Clark's killer.

Mellon's frustration mounted to the point where his wife began to worry about his health. His diet now consisted of black coffee and cigarettes, and he spent barely any time with his baby daughter. What Mellon's wife did not realize was that, unlike the hundreds of other cases he had worked on in his ten-year career, the hunt for the Boston Strangler totally consumed him. The case controlled his waking hours and invaded his dreams.

With Sophie Clark's murder, the Boston Strangler case moved into new territory. Clark was the first African American and the youngest woman to be killed thus far, and unlike the previous victims, she had not lived alone. Until now, many young women had been unconcerned with the strangler case because they did not consider themselves likely targets. But Sophie was a college student, and Boston was home to more college students than virtually any other place in the world. If anything positive could be taken from this heinous crime, Mellon hoped the murder of Sophie Clark would wake up young women across the city.

NEW YEAR'S EVE 1962

When Boston residents picked up their morning newspaper on New Year's Day 1963, they were jarred by a front-page story about a secretary strangled in the shadow of Fenway Park. Twenty-three-year-old Patricia Bissette had grown up in the small college town of Middlebury, Vermont. After finishing high school, she attended the University of Vermont for one year, but she yearned to breathe life outside northern New England and left Vermont for New York City and a job with American Airlines at Idlewild (now Kennedy) Airport. In New York Bissette began dating a co-worker, and a few months later they were engaged. But the fast-paced romance was too much too soon, and Patricia broke the engagement off and moved back to New England, where she found work as a secretary at a Boston firm called Engineering Systems.

On the morning of December 31, 1962, Bissette's boss, Jules Rothman, told the police, he drove to her apartment at 515 Park Drive to pick her up for work. He knocked on her apartment door at around 8:00 A.M., and when she did not answer, he waited several minutes and then left for work. But he was worried. Repeated phone calls to her apartment that day went unanswered. It was not like Bissette to miss work and not check in.

In the middle of the workday Rothman left his office and returned to Bissette's apartment. He and the building custodian tried unsuccessfully to open her door. Bissette's boss then climbed through her living room window. He found Bissette in bed with the sheet tucked under her chin. Several ligatures consisting of a white blouse and three stockings were knotted tightly around Bissette's neck. Her body was clothed only in a blue and red housecoat, which was pushed up above her breasts.

The medical examiner later determined that Bissette had had sexual intercourse shortly before her death. The examiner also discovered that Bissette was one month pregnant. A neighbor told police that she had heard screams coming from Bissette's apartment between three and four P.M. the day before her body was found. One of the items taken as evidence from the crime scene was an Easter card from Bissette's boss that read, "To Patsy . . . Love Jules." The man's assertion that the relationship was merely professional did not ring true. It soon became clear that Rothman was not only Patricia Bissette's boss; he also was her lover.

This detail would not have disturbed investigators if the boss had not already been married. In addition, Bissette's photo album had been stolen from her apartment, but the killer had left $125 on her dresser. Suspicion began to focus on Rothman. Was he the father of her unborn child? And had he killed her to cover up their affair? He was given a polygraph examination. The official report said, "Reactions exhibited on this chart indicate that he is not telling the truth." Bissette's boss had motive, and he had opportunity. Yet for reasons unknown, he was not arrested for the murder of his young lover. Following Bissette's murder, two reporters, Loretta McLaughlin and Jean Cole, wrote a four-part series on the case for the *Record American*. McLaughlin and Cole were convinced the murders had been committed by one man, whom they dubbed the "Boston Strangler."

MAY 9, 1963

After the Bissette killing Boston got a four-month reprieve from the strangler case. Spring was in full bloom. The baseball bats were swinging at Fenway Park, and Bostonians were enjoying walks through the Public Garden and Harvard Square. Winter had come and gone, but detective Jim Mellon had barely noticed. His mind was still focused on catching the killer or killers of the strangled women.

Then, on May 9, 1963, the body of twenty-six-year-old Beverly Samans was found inside her apartment on University Road in Cambridge. The tabloid *Record American* carried the headline "Cambridge Girl, 26, Strangled." But Beverly Samans had not only been strangled; she had also been stabbed seventeen times. The killer had plunged a knife into her left breast and slit her throat. In addition, a white scarf was knotted together with two nylon stockings and tied around her neck, and her hands were tied behind her back.

Beverly Samans was a graduate student at Boston University and an accomplished singer whose ultimate goal had been to sing mezzo-soprano at New York's Metropolitan Opera House. Friends said she had received obscene phone calls after her picture appeared in a local newspaper after one of her concerts. Samans, who worked part-time as a counselor for the mentally challenged at the nearby Fernald School, allowed some young Fernald residents inside her home, a fact that disturbed the police, who believed that many Fernald residents were potentially violent.

Shortly after Samans's murder, Daniel Pennachio, a former resident at Fernald, was arrested on a charge of lewd and lascivious behavior. While being interrogated for allegedly exposing himself in public, the twenty-eight-year-old Cambridge man startled police by confessing to Samans's murder, telling investigators he had stabbed the victim more than a dozen times. He also said he had put a gag in her mouth and a cloth over her head, details that had not been printed in the newspapers. According to Pennachio, Samans had invited him into her home, and they talked while she worked on a college thesis. Investigators remembered that page six of Samans's thesis had been in the carriage of her typewriter at the murder scene.

Despite his incriminating account of Beverly Samans's murder, police believed that Daniel Pennachio was delusional and not telling the truth. Thus, instead of being arrested for murder, he was fined for lewd behavior and released from jail. Weeks later, Pennachio was killed while diving with friends in the waters off South Boston. His death was ruled accidental, and no one has ever been charged with the murder of Beverly Samans.

SEPTEMBER 8, 1963

The city of Salem, famous for its seventeenth-century witch-hunts, lies fourteen miles north of Boston, along the state's rocky North Shore. On most other Sunday mornings, one of the city's residents, fifty-eight-year-old Marie Evelina Corbin, Evelyn to her friends, would have been attending mass, but that particular Sunday the mist off the ocean was so thick that Corbin thought it too risky to drive her car.

The night before, she and her beau, Robert Manchester, had shared a late dinner at Bianco's pizza stand along nearby Revere Beach. The two had been introduced by Manchester's mother and had been dating casually for a year and a half. Recently, Manchester had spoken of marriage, but Corbin was not interested. She had divorced in 1936 and rarely spoke of her former husband.

On the morning of September 8, 1963, Corbin had breakfast with Manchester's mother, who lived in the same apartment building as Corbin, and they made plans to get together for an early dinner with Manchester later that afternoon.

Robert Manchester left work and arrived at Corbin's apartment at approximately 1:15 P.M. that day. He rang her buzzer three times, but no one answered. He summoned his mother, who had a spare key, and the two entered the apartment, calling out Corbin's name. When they still received no reply, Manchester approached the bedroom door but found the handle stuck. Backing up a few steps, he rammed his body into the door, splitting the wood and forcing the door open. He found Corbin lying face up across her bed on top of the bed cover. Her left leg was hanging off the side of the bed. One stocking was tied around her left ankle, two more around her neck. Each stocking had been knotted in the front, one at the midline and the other just to the left of it. Her nightgown was ripped open, exposing her pubic area.

Though the hyoid bone in her neck was not broken, an autopsy revealed Corbin had been tied up, raped, and probably forced to perform oral sex on the killer. Semen was discovered in her mouth, and semen-stained tissues littered the bedroom floor. The apartment had not been ransacked, but the killer had rifled the victim's purse, scattering its contents across the floor.

Police believe the killer had entered Corbin's apartment through a window with a broken lock next to the fire escape. No neighbors said they had seen the killer enter the apartment, but many told stories that would disturb detectives for years to come. For instance, Allen Richard Spanks, who lived nearby, told the authorities that a man had knocked on his door the night before Corbin's murder and asked to see his wife, Betty. When Spanks told the man she was not home, the stranger said he had heard that Betty was looking for a new job and promised to return in a few hours to discuss a business opportunity. When Allen Spanks relayed the message to his wife, she was dumbfounded. She said she was very happy at work and had never told anyone she was looking for a new job. In any case, the stranger never returned. Spanks described the man as six feet tall, slim, with wavy, brown hair.

Another neighbor told investigators that on the morning of the murder, she had seen a man pacing back and forth outside Corbin's building, looking up at the apartments. "He was tall with brown, wavy hair and walked with a limp," she told the police.

A week after Corbin's murder, yet another neighbor, Pauline Marmen, called the police to say a man had appeared at her front door and said he had been told she was having a baby. When Marmen said it was not true, the man seemed disappointed and walked away. Marmen described the man as tall with brown hair. Despite repeated efforts, investigators never found the brown-haired suspect.

NOVEMBER 24, 1963

New Englanders were still reeling from the assassination of President John F. Kennedy. The city of Boston was paralyzed, with residents glued to their television sets as events unfolded more than a thousand miles away in Dallas. In the days after the assassination the homicide bureau of the Boston Police Department had a respite from the flood of calls from women claiming to have seen "a suspicious man." A silence had fallen over the city.

But not everyone was taking time out to grieve. Twenty-five miles north of Boston, in the gray mill town of Lawrence, investigators had another murder on their hands. The victim was Joann Graff, a twenty-three-year-old Sunday school teacher. Graff's friends had been concerned about her after she failed to show up at a dinner party the night before. The next day, when she did not appear at Sunday school, either, her friends called the police. An officer went to Graff's apartment at 54 Essex Street and found her there lying on her bed, her right leg dangling over the side and her right hand curled into a tight fist. The leg of her black leotard and two nylon stockings were tied in a knot around her neck. Her body had several bruises, and her bra, still in place, was soaked in blood. Joann Graff had also been raped, and her apartment had been torn apart, though an envelope with several dollars for a gas bill had been left on a counter. The landlord's wife told police that someone had been wandering the halls of the apartment building over the last few days.

While discussing the case with the Lawrence police, Jim Mellon uncovered a particularly disturbing fact. Graff's neighbor Kenneth Rowe had previously lived at 84 Gainsborough Street in Boston, across the street from Anna Slesers, the first victim. During interrogations by both Mellon and the Lawrence police officers, Rowe said he had lived on Gainsborough Street while attending Northeastern University and had recently moved to Lawrence for an engineering job. He also claimed he had never met Anna Slesers and barely knew Joann Graff. He did tell police that a man had been knocking on doors looking for Graff's apartment the day before her murder. Jim Mellon put Rowe's name on the expanding list of possible suspects.

By this time Mellon had been working full-time on the Boston Strangler case for eighteen months; nevertheless, no arrests had been made. Mellon believed he knew who some of the killers were, and he felt he had enough hard evidence to get arrest warrants in at least six of the cases, but his superiors did not agree. "What the hell more do they want?" he wondered.

The amount of paperwork collected in the Boston Strangler case was awesome. By the time the investigation ended, there were 37,500 pages. When the sheer volume finally became too much for detectives to sift through, the information gathered from various police departments was processed and fed into a computer. But the new technology was of little interest to Jim Mellon. He felt a personal connection each time he touched a file and looked at a victim's picture.

One evening after the Sullivan murder, Mellon sat in his office, reading through the case files. Before he knew it, the time was 1:30 A.M. Dropping Joann Graff's file and opening Mary Sullivan's, he stared at the young woman's picture and wondered, "When will the killing stop?"

Mellon closed the manila folder and hugged it to his chest, put his feet up on his desk, and went to sleep. He was awakened at 7:30 the next morning, when Phil DiNatale threw a copy of the *Record American* at his feet. "Look who wants to up the reward," DiNatale said. Mellon rubbed his eyes and grabbed the paper. Attorney General Edward Brooke had announced that he would ask the governor to double the reward, from $5,000 to $10,000, for information leading to the arrest of the strangler or stranglers. "Apparently, our boss doesn't think we can do the job," DiNatale said. Maybe he's right, Mellon thought to himself.

So far, authorities had questioned more than 3,000 people in connection with the Boston Strangler case. Jim Mellon and his task force comrades had read through the case histories of 2,300 known sex offenders and had brought in more than 400 suspects for interrogation. Along with the task force, the state had also established a medical-psychiatric committee to profile the perpetrator or perpetrators. Asked to consider whether the stranglings were all the work of one man, they came to a consensus that the older women had been victims of a single killer and that copycats had killed the younger victims, men who committed murder using various Boston Strangler techniques they had read about in the newspaper.

Attorney General Brooke also believed there were

several killers at large. In an interview with United Press International on August 19, 1964, Brooke theorized that Mary Sullivan was not a victim of the so-called "mad strangler." In fact, Brooke told reporters that he believed the real strangler had not struck since the murder of Jane Sullivan in 1962 and that he doubted the "mad strangler" was still on the streets. Perhaps the killer had taken his own life, Brooke said, or he could now be an inmate of a mental hospital or prison. As for the other six murders, Brooke said suspicion centered on "unstable individuals in the homosexual community of our society."

Jim Mellon knew this was not true and was angered that Brooke was talking to the press as if he were an expert on the case. The attorney general had never been involved in a murder investigation before, and the man he had chosen to lead the task force was a bow-tied real estate lawyer named John Bottomly, a longtime friend and former classmate of Brooke at Boston University School of Law.

Though he had never argued a criminal case, Bottomly, like Brooke, was active in Republican politics. Unlike the charismatic Brooke, however, the introverted Bottomly had not found political success as a Republican in the Democratic stronghold of Massachusetts, having lost his only campaign, a bid for the state senate, in the 1950s. Brooke told the press he had not chosen his friend for his investigative skills but because he was a great administrator, and that Bottomly's job was to coordinate information from the various police departments working on the strangler case.

Jim Mellon thought Brooke and Bottomly were using the Boston Strangler case for political ends. It was no secret that Brooke, the nation's only African American attorney general, was eyeing a seat in the United States Senate, where no black man had served since Reconstruction. If Brooke succeeded, his good friend John Bottomly might have a shot at the attorney general's office.

Nevertheless, Mellon discussed his theories about the Boston Strangler case with Bottomly on several occasions. Mellon believed an African American man working on the MacDaniels painting crew could have killed Anna Slesers and possibly Helen Blake. He also believed that a black man had strangled Sophie Clark. Mellon claims that Bottomly told him to keep those thoughts to himself. It would look very bad for Ed Brooke if the killers were black, Bottomly reportedly told Mellon. Bottomly suggested to Mellon that he did not want to complicate Brooke's political career by adding race as an issue in the strangler case. Mellon concluded that the case had become a political circus.

The political circus would soon become a full-blown carnival. John Bottomly came under harsh criticism from the task force when he added a psychic, Peter Hurkos, to the strangler team. A native of Holland, the fifty-two-year-old Hurkos was a former housepainter who claimed to have gained his psychic abilities after falling thirty-five feet from a ladder and fracturing his skull. When he regained consciousness three days later, Hurkos claimed, he pleaded with his doctor not to travel, but the doctor didn't heed the warning and died soon thereafter during a trip abroad. Hurkos first came to the United States in the 1950s, to help police in Miami catch a double murderer. He called himself "the psychic detective" and took credit for solving twenty-seven murders in seventeen countries.

Hurkos was in Los Angeles trying to close a deal for film rights to his life story when he was summoned to Boston. On the night of January 29, 1964, the Dutch psychic, accompanied by his six-foot, five-inch bodyguard, landed at the Providence, Rhode Island, airport, where he was met by

John Bottomly. Attorney General Brooke had not wanted Hurkos to fly into Boston's Logan Airport because he was worried about the publicity that might result from the psychic's involvement in the strangler case. Reporters might raise a fuss if they knew a self-professed mystic was being hired to help find the killers. Just to be safe, Brooke called a secret meeting with the Boston media, asking the reporters not to run stories about Hurkos's involvement unless it generated a break in the case. Such a request would be scoffed at today, but the reporters grudgingly agreed.

The day after the psychic arrived in town, investigators took boxes of evidence to Hurkos's room at the Battle Green Inn in Lexington, the site of "the shot heard round the world," which began the Revolutionary War. Hurkos, who checked in under a fake name, claimed he could see into a killer's mind by touching an object the killer had come in contact with. A handful of crime scene photographs lay face down in neat piles on the bed. Hurkos slowly ran his pudgy fingers over them. Soon he focused his attention on one stack. "This one, the top one. Show dead woman. Legs apart. I see her. Here, I show you." Hurkos, a tall and overweight man, fell to the carpet and demonstrated the position in which the victim had been left. A detective flipped the picture over and saw Anna Slesers lying on the floor with her legs spread apart in exactly the fashion that Hurkos had demonstrated.

Next, the detective pulled out several nylon stockings and scarves and placed them on the bed in front of the psychic. Hurkos once again ran his hands through the evidence. He claimed he saw a stick being stuffed inside a young woman's vagina. It was clear to the police officers in the room that Hurkos was talking about Mary Sullivan. "I see . . . I see a priest!" Hurkos shouted to the stunned detectives. The psychic then corrected himself and said the killer was not a priest but dressed like one and had spent time with many real priests. Hurkos was convinced that the killer once had worked in a seminary and now sold shoes door to door. A job like that would certainly give someone easy access to his victims' apartments.

Apparently investigators took these words to heart. According to Sidney Kirkpatrick (who wrote about this episode for the *Los Angeles Times Magazine*), they began to keep a close eye on fifty-six-year-old Daniel Moran, a shoe salesman. In his article titled "The Psychic, the Shoe Salesman, and the Boston Strangler," Kirkpatrick reports that Moran's family tried unsuccessfully to get him committed to a mental institution. Moran's own physician reportedly told police Moran was beset by the fear that he had become the strangler during mental blackouts. The shoe salesman lived in the shadow of Symphony Hall, a few blocks from where Anna Slesers and Sophie Clark had been strangled. Kirkpatrick also writes that Moran spent a brief period studying at St. John's Seminary after graduating from college. But besides a psychic's vision, the police had no evidence against the man. Daniel Moran never was charged with any of the strangler murders and died in 2001 in a Massachusetts mental hospital. As for Hurkos, he left Boston as quietly as he had arrived.

The cover on the Hurkos experiment was blown a few days later, however, after the FBI arrested Hurkos in New York City for having impersonated a federal agent. His involvement in the Boston Strangler case was revealed, and the media pounced on the story. In response to the resulting furor, Attorney General Edward Brooke assured the public that Hurkos had been paid for his cooperation not by the state but by two private citizens' groups.

Meanwhile, Jim Mellon continued to focus on the Mary Sullivan murder. Mellon thought there were two strong suspects. One was Mary's former boyfriend, Nathan Ward. Mellon had traveled to Cape Cod several times in the weeks following Mary's death. No one there had a good thing to say about Ward. In addition, Mellon had retrieved three buttons from a man's shirt that lay next to the toilet where the killer had attempted to flush a red ascot. A local tailor told Mellon they were of Asian design and probably came from Japan. Nathan Ward had been stationed in Japan while serving in the army.

Mellon was also disturbed by the fact that Ward married a woman he barely knew just three weeks after Mary Sullivan's murder. But what frustrated the investigator most was Ward's alibi. He swore he had been working at a Howard Johnson's restaurant the night of the murder. Yet Mary Sullivan's younger brother David claimed he had visited the restaurant twice that evening and could not find Ward. And while Ward's boss backed up the alibi, Mellon could not discount the fact that David had not seen Ward at the restaurant that night. Mellon had a feeling the boss was lying.

Another likely suspect was nineteen-year-old Joseph Preston Moss, Delmore's fiancé. Mellon felt the young man had been too cooperative with the police and reporters in the weeks following the murder. Moss would constantly call the Boston Strangler Task Force, asking for updates on the investigation. Moss also claimed to have visited the apartment the night of January 3, the night before the murder. He said when he knocked on the door and asked for Pat Delmore, Mary told him that she was visiting her parents. Moss told police he also heard a man's voice behind the door. Moss never saw the man, yet he described him to investigators as being tall with a protruding Adam's apple. In addition, Pat Delmore told the police that her apartment key had disappeared from her key chain the night before the murder. Delmore had spent much of that day with Moss. During a polygraph test requested by Mellon, the suspect denied having stolen his girlfriend's apartment key. The polygraph suggested he was lying. Mellon then asked Moss if he had anything to do with Mary Sullivan's murder, and he denied that. But again, the polygraph suggested he was lying. Moss's lawyer claimed the young man had not understood the questions and demanded that he be allowed to retake the polygraph test. Mellon granted the request, and Moss failed the test again. Besides his suspicious eagerness to assist the investigation and the two failed polygraph tests, another piece of evidence could also point to Moss. Two months after Sullivan's murder, her former roommate Pam Parker received a frightening phone call at her parents' home. "Is, is this Pam?" the caller asked. "Yes, it is," she answered. "I'm, I'm gonna do to you what I did to that Mary bitch," she was warned. The caller had a severe stutter. The only person Parker knew with such a speech impediment was Moss.

Of the two suspects, Nathan Ward seemed more likely. He certainly had a motive—jealousy—and had been verbally abusive toward Mary Sullivan. He had a fiery temper and was skilled in karate. It would not have been difficult for Ward to overpower Mary and choke her to death. The rare Japanese shirt buttons found at the crime scene also pointed to Nathan Ward, as did the ascot that had been cut up and stuffed into the toilet. Mary Sullivan's family and friends reported that she loved to buy Ward ascots as gifts. Perhaps the cut-up ascot was meant as a symbol of their fractured relationship. Joseph Preston Moss, on the other hand, had been interviewed outside Mary Sullivan's apart-

ment the night of the murder. A neighbor put a man match-
ing his description inside Mary's bathroom around the time
she was killed. And the results of the two polygraph tests
could not be ignored. If the killer was not Nathan Ward,
then Mellon was sure it was Preston Moss.

Mellon discussed his conclusions with John Bottomly
in December 1964. Bottomly shocked the investigator by
dismissing the evidence out of hand. Instead, he said the
task force was now focusing on Albert H. DeSalvo, an inmate at the Bridgewater Psychiatric Hospital. Mellon was
familiar with all the suspects in the Boston Strangler
case, but he had never heard of DeSalvo. Yet Bottomly
said there were rumors that DeSalvo was going to confess
to all of the murders.

During the same discussion, Bottomly asked Mellon
to help locate DeSalvo's family. It was known that he had
a young wife and two small children, but they had vanished from the family's home. "We know he had an apartment in Medford. Why don't you start there?" Bottomly
instructed. It took all of one afternoon for Mellon to find
Albert DeSalvo's wife. Driving to Medford, just a few
miles north of Boston, he inquired about the DeSalvo
children at a local elementary school. There he learned
that the records of Albert DeSalvo's daughter, Judy, had
been sent to an elementary school in Golden, Colorado.
DeSalvo's son, Michael, was too young to be enrolled in
school. Mellon returned to the task force office and
handed the information to Bottomly. "Pack your bags,
Jim. You're going to Colorado," he was told.

That night, Mellon took a commercial flight from
Logan Airport to Denver. During the long and bumpy
flight, Mellon chain-smoked Pall Malls and read the police file on Albert Henry DeSalvo.

3 : The Making of Albert DeSalvo

Albert Henry DeSalvo was born on September 3, 1931, on the outskirts of Boston in the port city of Chelsea. Chelsea, which covers roughly one square mile, is known as Boston's poor sister to the north. Today the city has a strong Latino population, but during the Great Depression it was a haven for destitute immigrant families from Italy and Ireland.

Like Mary Sullivan, Albert DeSalvo was the third of six children. His mother, Charlotte, was the daughter of a Boston firefighter. His father, Frank DeSalvo, was a plumber by training but a petty thief by trade. Albert was five years old when his dad took him to a store and taught him the art of shoplifting. When the elder DeSalvo wasn't training his son to become a modern-day Oliver Twist, he was treating his family to what seemed like a never-ending series of beatings. At age seven, young Albert could only look on as his drunken father punched Albert's mother in the mouth, scattering several of her teeth across the room. Frank DeSalvo then made his children watch as he snapped each of his wife's fingers, pulling them back until they broke.

His father beat not only Albert's mother but Albert as well. During one drunken rampage, Frank DeSalvo struck his young son across the back with a lead pipe. Officers from the Chelsea Police Department were constantly called in to break up domestic disputes in the DeSalvo household. They would usually find Frank De-Salvo drunk and screaming and a tearful Charlotte on the floor in a pool of her own blood. The elder DeSalvo was arrested many times for beating his wife, but she always took him back.

Money was extremely tight in the DeSalvo household. Although Charlotte did make some money as a seamstress, the DeSalvos were always on welfare. Frank De-Salvo spent his days drinking, his nights cavorting with women in the family's cramped Chelsea tenement. When Charlotte was out of the house, he brought prostitutes home and made his children watch while he had sex with them.

Albert later would claim that his father had once sold him and two of his sisters to a Maine farmer for nine dollars. According to this story, which was printed in several books as factual, the three children were held captive for several months until their father brought them home. But Richard DeSalvo, Albert's younger brother, says the claims of child slavery are altogether bogus. "Albert was a great storyteller," Richard says.

But even if the DeSalvo household was only half as bad as Albert claimed, it still was no place for a young boy to grow up. To escape his father's drunken beatings, young Albert ran away several times, usually sleeping under the docks in nearby East Boston, an area that was popular with the city's urchins. Here, under the massive wooden pylons, Albert DeSalvo would learn many skills from the other young ruffians.

DeSalvo was only twelve years old when he was arrested for beating up and stealing $2.85 from a neighborhood paperboy. Because he had no prior criminal record, he was given a suspended sentence. Five weeks later, after he and a friend broke into a house and stole jewelry worth $27, DeSalvo was caught with the stolen goods. The judge was not so lenient this time. DeSalvo was committed to the Lyman School for Delinquent Boys on December 29, 1943. Opened in 1848, the school was in 1943 the oldest reformatory in the United States and home to some eight hundred boys, most of them sentenced for violent crimes. The school taught the standard reading, writing, and arithmetic, but most left with what they may have deemed more useful skills. Lyman was a farm system for the streets, where boys would teach each other things like pickpocketing and the fastest way to hot-wire a car.

Albert DeSalvo would stay at the Lyman School for ten months. During this time, he was examined by a state psychiatrist, Dr. Doris Sidwell, who concluded that Albert was of normal intelligence. She also noted that the boy was deeply afraid of his father and was highly suggestible.

DeSalvo stayed out of trouble while at the Lyman School and was paroled in October 1944. That same year, his father vanished, taking with him the dark cloud that had hung over the family. Charlotte DeSalvo divorced him a year later. Thus, when Albert returned to his family in Chelsea, he no longer had to fear another violent eruption from his father.

Though he showed little aptitude for schoolwork, Albert DeSalvo received a different education outside the classroom, where he was romancing a thirty-five-year-old woman with a son his own age. And sex was not the only thing on DeSalvo's mind. It did not take long for him to return to his life as a thief. In 1946, he was arrested for stealing a car and sent back to the Lyman School.

Paroled in 1947, DeSalvo went back to school. This time, he took honest jobs, completed the ninth grade, and then tried to enlist in the United States Marine Corps, which rejected him for being overweight. DeSalvo then gave the U.S. Army a try. He passed the physical and took the oath to defend his country on September 16, 1948, at Fort Banks, Massachusetts. After basic training at Fort Dix, New Jersey, he was shipped overseas to Bremerhaven in Germany to join the 7720th European Command. DeSalvo was stationed at Headquarters Command for the fourteenth Armored Cavalry for three months before being transferred to Company G in Bamberg, Germany. There he served as an assault rifleman and light weapons infantryman. He also worked as a truck driver and motor messenger clerk. DeSalvo's superiors seemed to like the young man from Boston. His efficiency ratings ranged from "good" to "excellent." The army also awarded him a good conduct medal, the Army of Occupation Medal with a Germany Clasp, the National Defense Service Medal, and the Sharpshooter Badge with a Rifle Bar.

DeSalvo also found success in the military boxing ring. Standing five feet, ten inches and weighing by this time 155 pounds, the young DeSalvo was a fighter to be reckoned with, a veteran of many street wars in his hometown who had learned defensive moves from fighting with his own father. Crowned middleweight champion of Company G, he rose to the rank of sergeant but then was brought up on charges for failing to obey a lawful order from a noncommissioned officer. Tried by a summary court-martial on August 17, 1950, he was reduced to the rank of private and fined fifty dollars. Later that year, he was honorably discharged as a private first class and reenlisted for another tour of active duty.

It was during this time that DeSalvo met Irmgard Beck, a young German woman, at an army dance. Beck, who lived with her parents in nearby Frankfurt, spoke English and was captivated by the smooth-talking De-Salvo. The two were married on December 5, 1953. De-Salvo took his young wife back the states, where he was first stationed at Fort Hamilton, New York, and then at Fort Dix.

Married life proved difficult for Irmgard DeSalvo. Al-bert was constantly demanding sex, and when she said she was too tired for it, he sought excitement elsewhere. On January 5, 1955, DeSalvo was arrested for molesting a nine-year-old girl. The girl claimed that a soldier had knocked on her front door saying he was looking for a place to rent. After she allowed the man inside, she said, he attempted to fondle her chest and thighs. The girl's brother then came into the room, and the man fled. The brother told police that the suspect had a "Jimmy Durante nose." Around that time, a woman in the area reported a similar story about a man trying to talk his way into her home. She had written down his license plate number, which was Albert DeSalvo's. When DeSalvo was brought in for questioning regarding both cases, the nine-year-old identified him as the soldier who had attacked her. Denying the accusations, he was released on $1,000 bail. Fortunately for DeSalvo, the girl's mother feared the publicity the case would bring and refused to press the complaint. The charges were dropped, and the army did not take action.

Soon after, Irmgard DeSalvo discovered she was pregnant. The couple's first child, Judy, was born later that year. The birth of a daughter did little to ease the growing tension between Albert and Irmgard. Judy had been born with a rare pelvic disease and wore specially fitted removable casts in order to correct her crippled hip. Father Albert would tie the cast with big colorful bows to keep it tight around Judy's leg. It was something of a game between father and daughter.

In 1956, DeSalvo left the army. He moved his family to his hometown of Chelsea and began searching for work. But honest work did not supply the kind of money and excitement he sought. In early 1958, he was arrested for trying to break into a house during the night. Found guilty, he received a suspended sentence, but less than a month later, he was arrested in Chelsea for two daytime break-ins. DeSalvo told the judge he committed the crimes because he desperately needed money to buy his wife and daughter gifts for Valentine's Day. The story must have struck a chord because the judge gave DeSalvo another suspended sentence.

In the summer of 1959, DeSalvo and his wife returned to Germany. While there, Albert hatched a scheme that he would later use to great effect back in the United States. He visited U.S. Army post exchanges, claiming that he worked for *Stars and Stripes*, the army newspaper, and selected female employees for a phony "Best Sweetheart of All" contest, taking their measurements and promising first prize to the one who kissed him. This ploy kept him busy for the two months he and his wife and child spent in Germany. But by the fall, DeSalvo was back in Chelsea and back in trouble with the law. In October 1959, he was arrested for breaking and entering and again received a suspended sentence.

A healthy son was born to Albert and Irmgard in 1960. Michael's birth appeared to bring about a brief change in Albert. For the first time in his marriage, he came home at night for dinner and played with the kids. But the interlude did not last long. On St. Patrick's Day in 1961, while Irish-American revelers were cramming local pubs, DeSalvo attempted to break into a house in Cambridge. Spotted by two police officers, he fled on foot. After a brief chase, one of the cops, too exhausted to continue, fired a warning shot into the air, and DeSalvo froze. The officers found burglary tools in his jacket. After he was booked, DeSalvo was stripped down and thrown into a cell at Cambridge Police Headquarters, where he stayed for six days with barely anything to eat. He later told his family it was worst experience of his life.

While in custody DeSalvo offered the first of many startling confessions to police. He boasted to investigators that he was the mysterious "Measuring Man," the nickname given by police to an offender who had sexually assaulted several Cambridge women. The suspect would spot attractive women walking the streets around Harvard Square, follow them home, and then approach them at their doors. Passing himself off as a representative from a modeling agency, he'd ask the women if they ever dreamed about appearing in magazines or in the movies. Then he would take out his measuring tape and ask the aspiring models if he could size them up.

The Measuring Man played the perfect gentleman until he placed the tape measure around a woman's breasts, at which point he would grope and paw the victim. Most of the victims reacted angrily, and the Measuring Man would vanish quickly. The technique evolved from DeSalvo's beauty contest scam in Germany. Concerning the fact that he had approached young women near the campus of Harvard University, DeSalvo said, "I'm not good-looking. I'm not educated, but I was able to put something over on high-class people." Brought to trial in the Measuring Man case in May 1961, DeSalvo confessed to assaulting a dozen women but was found guilty only on two counts: assault and battery and lewdness. But this time there was no suspended sentence: DeSalvo was given two years at the Billerica House of Correction. The sentence was later reduced, and DeSalvo was freed in April 1962.

Once out of jail, the young father of two found steady work as a painter and laborer with the Munro Company in Chelsea. DeSalvo usually worked alone but would sometimes ask his younger brother, Richard, also a Munro employee, to help him. As the body count began to rise in the so-called Boston Strangler case, DeSalvo began to take notice. "He was always looking through the paper, reading about the murders," Richard recalls.

In September 1962 Albert got a new job, as a handyman for a Malden contractor, Russell Blomerth. His work put him in close contact with many housewives, likely a dangerous temptation for DeSalvo. Yet he doesn't seem to have acted on his sexual urges while doing jobs for Blomerth in various homes, even though he worked in close contact with several women, including Mrs. Miguel Junger of Belmont, Massachusetts, whose son Sebastian would grow up to write *The Perfect Storm*, a best-selling book about doomed Gloucester fishermen.

Albert DeSalvo's family would soon face a storm of its own, however. On the morning of October 27, 1964, the wife of a Boston University professor was startled awake by a strange man standing in her bedroom. In a soothing voice, the dark figure whispered, "You know me." Then, walking toward the bed, he told her he was a police officer and wanted to ask her a few questions. The frightened woman, leaping out of bed, noticed something shiny in the intruder's hand. It was a knife. Ordering her not to look at him, the intruder tied her hands, blindfolded her, and forced a gag into her mouth. Continuing to whisper, he said, "I won't hurt you." Then he lifted the woman's nightgown and began fondling her breasts, all the while asking for her forgiveness. The victim was certain she was about to be raped, but the intruder apologized once again and left the room as quietly as he had come.

At Cambridge Police headquarters, the shaken victim gave investigators a detailed description of her attacker. The suspect had slick black hair, a hooked nose, and a medium build. He was wearing some kind of work uniform consisting of a dark green shirt and green pants. Investigators were familiar with the suspect the victim had described. An alert had gone out to all law enforcement agencies in New England to be on the lookout for a sexual predator known as the Green Man, who was wanted in Connecticut for several sex assaults and break-ins. A Cambridge detective took one look at the police sketch and knew he had seen this man before. The detective didn't know him as the Green Man, though. He knew him as the Measuring Man.

In early November 1964, ten months after the murder of Mary Sullivan, Albert DeSalvo was positively identified by the Cambridge victim and placed under arrest. During his lengthy confession, DeSalvo admitted breaking into four hundred apartments in the greater Boston area and sexually assaulting three hundred women in Connecticut and Rhode Island. During one trip to Connecticut, DeSalvo claimed, he had assaulted four women in one day.

There is no question that Albert DeSalvo was a sexual predator, but the sheer volume of his claimed exploits should have raised eyebrows. If DeSalvo had committed three hundred sex assaults in Southern New England over a two-year period, one would think he had no time for anything else, including his job and his family. Yet DeSalvo's employer, Russell Blomerth, would later tell the police that DeSalvo was both hardworking and reliable. In any case, DeSalvo was booked on rape charges and shipped to Bridgewater State Hospital for a psychiatric evaluation.

Although he was a veteran of reform school and jail, nothing prepared DeSalvo for what he saw at Bridgewater. Called "the chicken coop" because of its unsanitary conditions, Bridgewater was a sprawling asylum for the insane and sexually dangerous. Built in the 1800s, the institution housed many of the region's forgotten souls. The forensic psychiatrist Ames Robey recalls a story he heard when he first started work at Bridgewater. "Lives were expendable at Bridgewater," he says. "The place was a real pit. Guards told me that back in the 1940s to amuse themselves they'd put a patient in a cell in his underwear. Then they'd open the windows and place bets on just how long it would take the patient to die from the cold."

Even in the 1960s, many cells at Bridgewater lacked toilets or beds. Inmates had to wrap dirty wool blankets around themselves and try to find a soft place on the cold concrete floor. Bridgewater, in short, resembled a medieval dungeon more than a hospital. Dr. Robey was the first to interview DeSalvo when DeSalvo arrived at Bridgewater. "I asked him how many women he had assaulted," Robey recalls. "Albert first said six hundred. Then, a bit later, it was up to a thousand."

Robey says he quickly realized his new patient had a vivid imagination. "He wanted to be important," Robey recalls. "If you said you broke into five homes, he'd say he broke into fifty." DeSalvo was a liar, Robey knew, but he also had an undeniable charm. "You had a tendency to like him," the psychiatrist says, "and the thought of him becoming violent just wasn't there." After meeting with DeSalvo once a day for the thirty-five-day court-ordered observation period, Robey concluded that DeSalvo had a sociopathic personality but was competent to stand trial in the Green Man case.

In December 1964, DeSalvo was sent to the East Cambridge jail to await trial. Once there, his cocksureness disappeared, and he began acting like some of the mentally ill patients he'd seen at Bridgewater, telling his jailers he heard voices and also that he thought of killing himself. After one month in the jail, he was returned to Bridgewater.

In February 1965, DeSalvo would get his first hearing in front of a judge on the Green Man charges. Robey, the only witness testifying on his behalf, said DeSalvo's condition had grown worse and he was no longer competent to stand trial. DeSalvo then took the stand and told the judge he was competent to stand trial, but he needed better psychiatric care than Bridgewater could provide. De-Salvo maintained he was treated like an animal and that doctors at the hospital were not interested in helping him gain control over his powerful sexual urges. The judge was not swayed, and DeSalvo was sent back to Bridgewater.

Robey, who continued to treat DeSalvo, found himself awed by the man's memory. "He had a photographic memory," Robey says. "I'd bring him into a room full of doctors, and he'd tell us the exact seats we sat in two weeks before." Robey also noticed that DeSalvo had struck up a friendship with George Nassar, another inmate.

Nassar had been sent to Bridgewater for observation after his arrest for the cold-blooded murder of a gas station attendant in Andover, an upscale Boston suburb near Lawrence, where another Boston Strangler victim, Joann Graff, was killed. On September 29, 1964, the attendant had been checking gas pumps when a man in a tan trench coat came up behind him and plunged a knife into his back. Irving Hilton, the victim, begged for his life, but to no avail. The attacker pulled a .22 automatic from his trench coat and shot Hilton six times. At that moment, Rita Boute pulled into the service station with her four-teen-year-old daughter. When Boute heard the gunfire, she and her daughter ducked beneath the steering col-umn. The killer, who had seen the car pull in, calmly walked up and stared at the terrified pair. He tried to open the car door, but, finding it locked, he instead tried to fire a shot through the windshield. Fortunately, no bullets were left in the gun. The man in the tan trench coat got into his car and sped away.

Rita Boute gave a near-perfect description of the killer. She said he had wavy, brown hair, rigid cheekbones, and black, soulless eyes. A police artist drew a picture that bore a striking resemblance to George Nassar, a Lawrence native who had been released from prison in 1962 after serving time for murder.

Nassar had been arrested at age fifteen for fatally shooting a grocery store owner during a holdup and sentenced to thirty years to life. While in prison the young man showed a keen aptitude for learning and convinced local ministers that he had changed his ways. The ministers petitioned for Nassar's release and he was freed after serving almost fourteen years. When they compared Nassar's mug shot to the police sketch, investigators were sure he was the one who had murdered the gas station attendant. They traced Nassar to an address in Boston's South End, only a few blocks from several Boston Strangler crime scenes. When they searched Nassar's apartment for evidence in the gas station murder, they found a police and a doctor's uniform in his bedroom closet. Nassar could have used these disguises to gain access to the strangling victims' apartments.

Ames Robey interviewed Nassar when he arrived at Bridgewater. "He had a real hatred toward women," recalls Robey, who already had interviewed several suspects in the Boston Strangler case and had helped the task force create a psychological profile of the killer. According to Robey, "Albert DeSalvo did not fit the profile at all. But George Nassar fit it ideally. He had a real hatred of women and was prone to homicidal urges." In any case, after meeting Nassar, DeSalvo underwent a personality change. Robey says that before Nassar arrived at Bridgewater, DeSalvo was quite friendly with the other inmates and even the guards. But after Nassar arrived, he behaved as if he and Nassar were the only two inmates in the hospital. The two spent most of their time together, in the common room in the facility. "The other inmates knew they were not to be disturbed, unless you wanted to be the victim of an accident, like falling in the shower and breaking your neck," says Robey. When hospital guards got too close, the two would immediately stop talking. One former Bridgewater inmate says he heard the men discussing the Boston Strangler case. The inmate remembers Nassar quizzing DeSalvo about details, after which the pair would go over the story again and again. "DeSalvo was a punk, but I was scared shitless of George," the former inmate says.

The once chatty DeSalvo also stopped talking to Robey, but in this case, the psychiatrist claims DeSalvo was merely acting on the advice of his new lawyer, a brash young attorney named F. Lee Bailey.

Francis Lee Bailey was born in Waltham, Massachusetts, in 1933. His father was in advertising, and his mother was a nursery school teacher. Lee, a fair athlete and a star pupil, finished high school at age sixteen and entered Harvard University. After Harvard, where Bailey was an average student, he joined the U.S. Navy and enrolled in naval aviation school. Finishing there, he transferred to the U.S. Marine Corps with his heart set on flying Sabre Jets. However, when his squadron's chief legal advisor was killed in a plane crash, Bailey was ordered to fill the position. His chance of becoming a pilot was over, but his legal career was born.

Bailey worked on several cases during his two remaining years of military service. Sometimes he worked as a prosecutor, other times as a defense attorney, all the while soaking up the protocol and nuances of military law. After his discharge, he worked as an investigator for a Boston lawyer and put himself through law school at

Boston University. He graduated in 1960 and hung out his shingle that fall. Bailey quickly built a reputation around local courthouses as a lawyer willing to use any method at his disposal to help his client and promote himself. Working hard to become a superstar lawyer, even more famous than Clarence Darrow had been, Bailey hired a driver and was the first attorney to customize his automobile with a swivel chair in front on the passenger side so he could swivel around to chat with reporters tagging along in the backseat.

Bailey's first high-profile case came in 1961, when he got a call from the brother of Sam Sheppard. Sam Sheppard, a physician, was serving ten years in an Ohio prison for the murder of his pregnant wife, who had been bludgeoned to death in the couple's Cleveland area home in 1954. Sheppard claimed he had walked in on the killer, who had knocked him unconscious with a blow to the head, but prosecutors argued he had murdered his wife after she discovered he was having an affair with a medical technician. During Sheppard's trial, the jurors were allowed to read every salacious detail of the affair in the newspapers and even permitted to talk with reporters. The case, which made headlines across the country, would later spawn the television series *The Fugitive*.

F. Lee Bailey filed an appeal of Sheppard's conviction, claiming the defendant had not received a fair trial because the jury had been polluted by the publicity surrounding the case. A federal judge agreed and released Sheppard in the summer of 1964, pending a retrial. The case was retried two years later, in the fall of 1966. This time, with Bailey as his defense attorney, Sam Sheppard was found not guilty of his wife's murder.

Bailey claims he first heard about Albert DeSalvo

from his client George Nassar in March 1965. In his book *The Defense Never Rests,* Bailey relates that Nassar mentioned DeSalvo and the possibility of making money from the Boston Strangler case. "If a man was the strangler," George Nassar said, "the guy who killed all those women, would it be possible for him to publish his story and make some money with it?" "I had to smile," Bailey writes. "It's perfectly possible to publish, but I wouldn't advise it. I suspect that a confession in book form would be judged completely voluntary and totally admissible. I also suspect that it would provide the means by which the author would put himself in the electric chair."

Bailey claims Nassar also pleaded with him to travel to Bridgewater State Hospital to meet DeSalvo, after which Bailey contacted the Boston Police Department and asked for information to help him determine whether DeSalvo was involved in the Boston Strangler case. Bailey writes that police gave him answers to five questions that only the killer could know. Bailey says he quizzed DeSalvo on those unreleased crime scene details, and that DeSalvo passed that test.

Knowing the publicity that was likely to result from this sensational case, Bailey advised DeSalvo's wife to take her young children as far away from Boston as possible. Irmgard DeSalvo told Bailey she had a sister living in Colorado, and Bailey gave her money for three plane tickets.

4 : Snow Job

Special Officer Jim Mellon knew something was amiss with the DeSalvo case because Albert DeSalvo was simply too eager to tell his story. Mellon hoped Irmgard DeSalvo could fill some of the holes in the mystery.

Arriving in Colorado, Mellon rented a car and drove to the small community of Golden, tucked deep into the Rocky Mountains. Irmgard and the two children were living in a trailer park just outside town. Mellon had rehearsed his approach to Irmgard. He would offer his irresistible Irish smile and a few sympathetic words, in the hopes she would talk to him. Knocking gently on the aluminum door, he watched as she nervously approached. "Who are you? Why have you come here?" Irmgard said with a thick German accent. Her eyes darted across the snow-covered parking lot, looking for newspaper reporters, whom Bailey had warned her against. But when Mellon took out his police badge from his coat pocket to identify himself, Irmgard quickly ushered him inside.

Mellon was pleased to see that the children were not

home. "I'd like to speak with you about your husband," he told her. Looking annoyed, Irmgard flipped the bangs of her platinum blonde hair off her forehead. "I don't know what he's thinking," she said. "He's always got some scheme to make it rich. He's always trying to be the big man." Irmgard paced back and forth in the small trailer.

Mellon tried to ease the tension. "Just between you and me, dear," he said with a wink, "I don't think he's the strangler, either." He then asked Irmgard to call her husband at Bridgewater State Hospital, saying, "Just ask him what he's up to. Albert could be setting you and the children up for a great fall."

Irmgard complied with Mellon's suggestion. Hearing her husband's voice for the first time in weeks, she began to scream, "Why are you telling everyone you're the Boston Strangler? This is crazy!"

Jim Mellon leaned closer to listen to Albert's reply.

"Just calm down," Albert said. "Bailey's got everything taken care of. Look, there's a lot of money to be made here. Just keep quiet, and everything will be fine."

"But there's a police officer here from Boston asking questions. How can you tell me everything is going to be fine? You're telling people lies, you're telling them you're the Boston Strangler," Irmgard shouted into the phone.

"Relax, Irm, I never told anyone I was the strangler. Put that cop on the phone," Albert demanded.

Mellon put the receiver up to his ear.

"Who the hell are you?" DeSalvo inquired.

Mellon thought for a second and then replied, "I'm the guy that's gonna expose you for the fraud that you are."

"Put my wife back on the phone," DeSalvo ordered. He then asked Irmgard to continue the conversation in German, and the couple talked for several more minutes. Mellon had no idea what they were discussing, but it was not pleasant, judging by the harsh tone of Irmgard's voice.

After she hung up, Mellon thanked her for her time and promised that he'd stay in touch. By now Mellon was certain that DeSalvo was no serial killer. But why would Albert DeSalvo confess to crimes he did not commit? In part it was his wish for fame and money. Not only did De-Salvo dream of a lucrative book deal, but he and his friend George Nassar also hoped to cash in on a reward. The Attorney General was offering $10,000 for information that would lead to the Boston Strangler's arrest. The two inmates believed that ten grand was being offered for each victim, bringing the total to $110,000. (This was un-true.) Nassar would turn DeSalvo over to the authorities, and the two of them would split the reward.

But fame and money were not the only factors in De-Salvo's actions. He told his family and F. Lee Bailey that he was afraid to go to prison. Bailey convinced DeSalvo that by confessing to the stranglings, he would be spared prison and be sent to a secure psychiatric hospital, where his criminal mind would be studied.

When Jim Mellon returned to Boston, he was deter-mined to pursue Joseph Preston Moss, the man he now considered the prime suspect in Mary Sullivan's murder. Moss had recently dropped out of Boston University, a move his friends blamed on the stress of the investiga-tion. Believing the young man was about to crack, Mel-lon made a formal request to John Bottomly to place a wiretap on Moss's home phone. He thought he would have no trouble convincing Bottomly, who had also called Moss the number one suspect in Sullivan's murder. He told Bottomly about the trip to Colorado and the bizarre phone call between the DeSalvos. "He's just in it for the money. I don't care what he claims to know about the murders, this guy is a con man," Mellon argued. Bottomly did not share Mellon's skepticism about DeSalvo. "We're going with DeSalvo and that's it," Bottomly said. Mellon continued to argue his point, but his superior refused to budge, and Mellon realized that the play had already been set in motion. Albert DeSalvo would not only confess to Mary Sullivan's murder, he would confess to all the murders, thereby tying this incredible case up in a neat bow. Soon after his meeting with Bottomly, Jim Mellon resigned from the Boston Strangler Task Force.

While cleaning out his desk at the task force office, he opened Mary Sullivan's case file one last time, stared at the girl's picture, and said softly, "I'm sorry, Mary." As punishment for quitting the task force, Mellon was taken out of plainclothes and put back in uniform. One day he was investigating one of the biggest murder cases in history, and the next he was on Dorchester Avenue, frisking a shoplifter for a stolen candy bar. Nevertheless, he has never regretted quitting the task force and at the time was disgusted with his task force colleagues for not quitting also.

Albert DeSalvo's confessions to the Boston Strangler murders were spread out over the next several months. His first interrogator was F. Lee Bailey, who claimed he had received information from DeSalvo about the murders that proved his guilt. The following transcript comes from a taped conversation between Bailey and DeSalvo at Bridgewater State Hospital on March 6, 1965, about the murder of Anna Slesers:

BAILEY: What floor was the apartment on?
DESALVO: The top floor.

BAILEY: Do you know how many flights that was from the street?

DESALVO: Probably four to five, or five to six. I think it was five. I'm not sure.

BAILEY: And how did you gain entrance to the apartment?

DESALVO: I knocked on the door and I . . . she allowed me in. . . . I talked to her about some work I had to do in the apartment. She had a blue robe on; undoubtedly she was getting ready for a bath, because the light was on in the bathroom and there was water, I'm pretty sure, in the bathtub. And as she walked, and I was behind her, I hit her on the head with this object I had in my hand, and she fell. And as she fell, I reached over the back of her and put my arms around her neck, and we fell together on the floor. [DeSalvo goes on to say that he lay with Slesers on the floor until she was helpless in his arms.] The blood was going all over me, and when I got up and looked, I was full of blood on my black and white jacket. I had her [bath]robe belt, a blue one, and I put it around her neck and tied it and left it on her. She was still alive, and I had intercourse with her.

BAILEY: And when you left her, how was she dressed?

DESALVO: I left her lying on the floor with her legs wide open about five feet from the bathroom. I went to the bathroom and washed up afterwards.

BAILEY: What was the position of her robe?

DESALVO: Open.

BAILEY: Not on?

DESALVO: No, I don't think . . . no, her arms were still in her sleeves.

BAILEY: Did she have anything on under the robe?

DESALVO: Nothing.

BAILEY: Can you describe her physically in any way?

DESALVO: Flat busted, a very small thin woman.

BAILEY: How tall?

DESALVO: About five feet five, or five four.

BAILEY: What color hair did she have?

DESALVO: Dark brown and very short.

BAILEY: Did she have any marks or scars that you recall?

DESALVO: No I don't [recall].

BAILEY: And where was she bleeding from?

DESALVO: The back of her head or on top.

BAILEY: And when she was lying down on the floor, as she bled, which way was her face . . . toward the ceiling or upside down?

DESALVO: That I don't remember.

BAILEY: Was there a pool of blood anywhere on the floor?

DESALVO: No, it was only on me.

BAILEY: Do you remember how many rooms [there] were in the apartment?

DESALVO: There was a large one, the bathroom, and the kitchen . . .

BAILEY: And the bathroom?

DESALVO: Very small.

BAILEY: And as you went into the apartment, which way did you turn to the bathroom?

DESALVO: Left, to the bathroom.

BAILEY: And can you see the bathroom when you're at the door?

DESALVO: I don't think so.

BAILEY: Any other recollection of what the interior of the bathroom was like, colors, decorations?

DESALVO: No, it was like a yellow . . . maybe I'm wrong.

BAILEY: Now, when you left the apartment; how long were you there first?

DESALVO: Twenty minutes. It was a sunshiny day . . . A very nice day.

BAILEY: All right. And when you left the apartment, did you take anything with you?

DESALVO: Twenty dollars.

BAILEY: Anything else?

DESALVO: No . . . yes, oh yes, I'm sorry. I did take something else. Because of the . . . I went in the bathroom and washed all the blood off, took my shirt off and my jacket. I went looking for something to put over me and I found a light tan . . . like a raincoat . . . and it was very short on my arms, but I thought I oughta have something to cover me to walk out of the building without a shirt on. So I did, and I bundled up my bloody clothes, and I put the bundle in some [kind of a bag].

BAILEY: Where did you go when you left the apartment?

DESALVO: I went downstairs . . .

BAILEY: Did you lock the door when you left?

DESALVO: Yes . . . I closed it, and it probably snapped locked.

BAILEY: Did you check it?

DESALVO: No, I didn't.

BAILEY: You still had gloves?

DESALVO: Yes.

BAILEY: Did you take them off?

DESALVO: As soon as I got out the door.

BAILEY: Now, was your appearance in that neighborhood much like it is today? If someone had seen you, would you look the same, or was your hair different?

DESALVO: My hair was very long; it was combed to both sides, waved to both sides.

BAILEY: Was it the same shade as it is now?

DESALVO: Oh no, [I had] thick black hair.

BAILEY: Well, your hair is now brown, I take it.

DESALVO: But when I have oil in it, my hair looks black.

BAILEY: Oh, I see. Okay. Now, again. The knot . . . how did you tie this knot in the cord?

DESALVO: I gave it two turns . . . the first one . . .

BAILEY: Two loops and then tightened it?

DESALVO: Tightened it, and then the other one one time. But on this one, I don't know when I did it, if it got tangled into a bow or not or what. But I do know that it is possible that a bow was made, but not purposely.

BAILEY: Now, on what area of her neck would the knot be; front, side, or back?

DESALVO: Front.

BAILEY: Under the chin?

DESALVO: Yes.

It could be argued that Albert DeSalvo assuredly was inside Anna Slesers's apartment on the June day when she was murdered in 1962, but serious questions arise when you look at the sources of information DeSalvo had available to help him paint a picture of the murder scene. A description of Slesers's physical appearance had been in the newspaper, along with her vital statistics, such as her height and weight. That Slesers was getting ready for a bath at the time she was killed had also been printed in the *Record American,* and the color of the woman's housecoat had been mentioned three times, in both Boston newspapers. What is more, Ames Robey, the psychiatrist, has pointed out repeatedly, Albert DeSalvo had a very good memory.

But if Albert DeSalvo fed off the newspapers to help put together a believable confession, where did he get the details of facts that were not printed in the newspapers? Mellon believes he knows the answer. In the months after quitting the task force, Mellon tried to get the Boston Strangler case out of his mind. But one evening in the summer of 1965, Mellon received a telephone call from the secretary at the task force. "What do you want from me?" Mellon asked. "Take me back to the first strangler murder, the murder of Anna Slesers," she replied. "What color was the couch in Slesers's apartment?" Mellon hesitated, his mind racing. Why would she need this information? "Oh, my God, they're feeding these details to DeSalvo," Mellon thought to himself. So he lied and told the secretary that the couch was blue with orange trim. There is no way to determine whether this incorrect information was given to DeSalvo, however, since a description of Slesers's couch was not listed in the transcript of the confession.

Another indication of Albert DeSalvo's mendacity is that he got into trouble when he went off script. DeSalvo told Bailey that once he left Selsers's apartment, he went to an army-navy store around the corner and bought a new shirt, because his own was covered with blood. But there was no army-navy store in Slesers's Back Bay neighborhood. The last clothing store in the area had gone out of business in February 1962, four months before Slesers was killed.

By August 1965, there had not been a strangling since Mary Sullivan's, more than a year and a half before. For months after Sullivan's slaying, newspaper columnists had blasted the authorities for their inability to solve this case. But now the columnists moved on to other, fresher topics. Still, the Boston Strangler Task Force was viewed as the laughingstock of Massachusetts law enforcement, and John Bottomly had to do something drastic to change this perception and thereby ensure his political future.

On August 11, 1965, Bottomly traveled to Bridgewater State Hospital to interview Albert DeSalvo. More seasoned members of the task force opposed the move because Bottomly had no experience in interrogation. As for Bailey, he insisted on one stipulation: any confession DeSalvo made would not be used against him in court. Bottomly readily agreed, a decision that would haunt the case for decades to come.

Bottomly met DeSalvo in a small room at the hospital. Sitting next to DeSalvo was an attorney, George McGrath. A judge had ruled that DeSalvo was not competent to handle his own affairs, and McGrath, a friend of Bailey's, had been chosen as his legal guardian. Bottomly had brought with him a few legal notepads and several pens as well as reels of audiotape for his tape recorder. He also had a folder stuffed with crime scene photos. In standard police interrogations, suspects are never allowed to look through pictures of the crime scene. Doing so would give the suspect added information about the murder. But Bottomly said that showing the photos to DeSalvo would jog his memory. Laying some photos of the Anna Slesers murder scene on the table, Bottomly hit the record button on his tape machine and began to interview the suspect. DeSalvo told Bottomly the same things he had told Bailey about Slesers's murder. They quickly moved to Nina Nichols, Boston Strangler victim number two.

DeSalvo's confession to the Nichols murder got off to a rocky start, however. DeSalvo told Bottomly her apartment was directly across from a fire door leading from the stairway. A later visit to the building by investigators proved this to be inaccurate. DeSalvo did tell Bottomly that Nichols had come to the door in her bathrobe, which was true. But this fact had been printed in the newspaper. He also said the victim lived on the fourth floor, that she had been wearing tennis shoes, and that the killer had left her lying on the floor of the apartment. But all these details had also been chronicled in the newspaper. DeSalvo also stated that he had ejaculated inside Nichols's vagina. But again, the fact that Nichols had been raped was highly publicized, and there was no mention of sperm inside the vagina in Nichols's autopsy report. DeSalvo also said, incorrectly, that the victim had been wearing stockings at the time she was killed. In addition, DeSalvo said that Nichols had scratched him and drawn blood with her fingernails. But the medical examiner had found no trace of skin or blood underneath her fingernails.

Bottomly next questioned DeSalvo about the death of Helen Blake, who had been murdered the same day as Nichols, a few miles north of Boston in the city of Lynn. When asked to describe the exterior of Blake's apartment building, DeSalvo said its front was sided with hard oak. The outside of Blake's apartment building, however, was not wood but concrete halfway up; above that was brick. DeSalvo also told Bottomly that there was some kind of name on the front door, like The Manor. This statement also proved false. Moreover, in describing the layout of Blake's apartment, DeSalvo placed the bathroom to the left of the front door, though it was actually on the right as you walked into the apartment.

When Bottomly asked DeSalvo how he had gained access to Blake's apartment, DeSalvo said, "I told her I was going to do some work for her on the ceilings. She was in the midst of shaking out some rugs when she opened her door. The rugs were on the window in the room.

"She was bent facing the bed, and I put my arms around her neck, but she went into a dead faint. A little blood was dripping from her nose, and she wore glasses," DeSalvo said. He maintained that he had taken off

Blake's pajama bottoms and had sex with her while she was unconscious. After raping Blake, DeSalvo claimed, he had grabbed a bra from her dresser and wrapped it around her neck. DeSalvo also said he tied a nylon stocking in three loops around her neck.

Bottomly's deficient interrogation skills are evident from his questions to DeSalvo about Helen Blake's clothes.

BOTTOMLY: Do you remember the material that the pajamas were made of?
DESALVO: Yes, well no, it wasn't . . . it was, uh, cotton.
BOTTOMLY: You think it was striped?
DESALVO: Yes.
BOTTOMLY: White with a colored stripe?
DESALVO: I'd almost swear it was stripes or some little design.

In this exchange Bottomly was obviously leading De-Salvo. There is no way of knowing whether DeSalvo could have accurately described Blake's striped pajamas because his interrogator was dropping hints about their design. And DeSalvo got many other details wrong. Though he told Bottomly he'd raped the victim, vaginal and rectal swabs showed no traces of sperm. Though he stated that he had bitten Blake hard on her breast, the autopsy report doesn't mention any marks on the victim's breasts. Though he also claimed to have bitten Blake's stomach in several places, the medical examiner had found no sign of this during his autopsy, either.

The inaccuracies do not end there. DeSalvo told Bottomly, incorrectly, that windows in Blake's apartment had been partially open, with rugs hanging out of them. In fact all the windows in Blake's apartment had been shut;

two rugs were found folded inside the front door of the apartment. When asked by Bottomly to describe Blake's living room, DeSalvo spoke at great length about a white mantelpiece with pictures on it. There was no mantelpiece in the apartment.

The answers to most of the questions he got right involved matters that had been widely publicized in the newspapers, such as the fact that Blake's killer had removed her pajama bottoms but left her top on. DeSalvo also flip-flopped on some of his answers. Initially, he told Bottomly that he had left Helen Blake on her back on the bed. Weeks later, DeSalvo told Bottomly, correctly, that Blake had been left on her stomach, with her feet hanging straight down off the bed. Did Albert DeSalvo, a man with a photographic memory, forget how he had killed Helen Blake? Or was he being tutored throughout his confession to provide the right answers?

Next on the list of victims was Ida Irga. DeSalvo told Bottomly, "I just picked her bell at random. I rang three other bells, and whoever came to the door, that's how it happened. She was the first to answer. She argued with me at first. I said I wanted to do some work in the apartment, and she didn't trust me because of the things that were going on, and she had a suspicion of allowing anybody into the apartment without knowing definitely who they were. I talked to her very briefly and told her not to worry. I said, 'If you don't trust me, I'll just come back tomorrow.' I started walking downstairs, and she said, 'Well, come on in.' I walked in with her, and we went into the bathroom, where I was supposed to look at a leak there at the window. When she turned, I put my arms around her neck and . . ."

DeSalvo went on to say that he had strangled Irga, had had intercourse with her limp body, and ejaculated inside her. There are many discrepancies between his account of the Irga murder and details from the crime scene and autopsy. First, the autopsy showed no trace of semen. Further, though DeSalvo claimed the victim had been wearing a black and white checkered bathrobe the night she was killed, Irga's housecoat was brown with white polka dots. When describing how he had killed the woman, DeSalvo told Bottomly he had strangled her manually from behind. In reality, Irga's killer had choked her to death with a pillowcase. DeSalvo did accurately describe Irga's apartment building and the general layout of the flat, but the psychiatrist Ames Robey dismisses claims that DeSalvo committed the murders. "Just because he knew what the apartments looked like doesn't mean he was the strangler," Robey argues. "Albert told me that he had visited several of the crime scenes because he was so fascinated by the case. As a maintenance man, he had apartment keys to half the buildings in Boston." What is more, task force records indicate there was a newspaper story or crime scene photo to account for almost every correct answer DeSalvo gave to questions about the Irga murder. But, though DeSalvo's confession to the murder of Ida Irga was riddled with holes, Bottomly failed or refused to see them.

The discrepancies in DeSalvo's confession to the murder of the next victim are even more disturbing. When asked to provide the date and time when he killed Jane Sullivan, DeSalvo could not answer. "I don't know, see," he said. "When this certain time comes upon me, it's a very immediate thing. When I get up in the morning and I get this feeling and . . . instead of going to work, I might make an excuse to my boss and I'd start driving. I'd start in my mind . . . building this image up, and that's why I found myself not knowing where I was going." Clearly, DeSalvo was a professional confessor. If he could not answer a question, he would change the course of the conversation.

Granted, DeSalvo accurately described Sullivan's apartment building on Columbia Road in Dorchester, but he admitted that he'd been to the building several times over the years. Further, his description of the murder scene was inaccurate. DeSalvo claimed that the floor in Sullivan's apartment had been covered in a thick layer of white dust. The crime scene photos show that the flat had been swept clean. DeSalvo said he had left the victim in the bathtub facing the wall. Sullivan had been discovered in her bathtub, as reported in the newspaper, but she was not facing the wall. Rather, she had been placed face down in six inches of water, her body in a crouching position.

DeSalvo also said he had tried to strangle Jane Sullivan manually, but then his hands got tired, and he grabbed a broom handle and wedged it under her chin. According to DeSalvo the makeshift garrotte had had little effect on the victim, so he threw it on the floor and left it there. The fact that Sullivan was attacked with a broomstick had appeared in several newspaper accounts. However, the broomstick had not been left on the apartment floor. Whoever murdered Jane Sullivan had taken the time to store the weapon neatly back in the broom closet.

Bottomly's interrogation of DeSalvo would last another thirty hours over a number of days. The days spent sitting across from Bottomly and his tape machine began to wear on DeSalvo; his mistakes became more glaring over time.

BOTTOMLY: What was the next door you knocked at?
DESALVO: Sophie Clark, and she was wearing a light, flimsy housecoat. And she was tall, well built, about 36-22-37. Very beautiful.

BOTTOMLY: How old?

DESALVO: To me she looked twenty, and she was, I think, twenty and . . .

BOTTOMLY: Describe her apartment. What kind of door did it have?

DESALVO: It was a yellowish door . . . and she was very, she didn't want to let me in, period, because her room-mates weren't in there at the time and they were going to be there very shortly. I said something about I would set her up in modeling and photography work, and I would give her anywhere from twenty to thirty-five dollars an hour for this type of modeling. And she invited me in to talk to her . . .

BOTTOMLY: How long did you talk with her?

DESALVO: Five minutes.

BOTTOMLY: Where was she when you attacked her?

DESALVO: [The] parlor.

BOTTOMLY: In the parlor. The moment you walked in from the front door?

DESALVO: Yes.

BOTTOMLY: How did you do it?

DESALVO: I gathered her around the back, and she was so tall that we fell back into this thing that was . . .

BOTTOMLY: The settee [couch].

DESALVO: Yes, where they had these . . .

BOTTOMLY: Pillows?

DESALVO: Pillows. And, for as strong as the girl was, she passed out right away.

BOTTOMLY: Uh-huh. Did you scissors her?

DESALVO: Yes, that's what did it. And she was knocked out. I tied her up. . . .

This exchange draws particular criticism from law enforcement officers. After reading the transcript, Sergeant Conrad Prosnewski, a long-serving veteran of the Salem, Massachusetts, Police Department, said it is clear that Bottomly had never conducted an interrogation before. "You never give this kind of information to a suspect. [Bottomly] lets DeSalvo know there were pillows on the couch, and he strongly indicates to his suspect that the victim was struck in the head with a pair of scissors," Prosnewski points out.

As the interrogation continued, DeSalvo said, "No, I'm wrong there. On Sophie Clark, this Negro girl, I did not have to tie her at all. She's the one who . . . was menstruating very lightly. I remember when I . . . she had the white thing on. I ripped that off her and threw it behind a chair."

BOTTOMLY: How did you remove this thing?

DESALVO: I just grabbed it.

BOTTOMLY: What material was it made of?

DESALVO: The same as any Kotex, that's it.

BOTTOMLY: After you took that off, where was she now?

DESALVO: Lying on the floor.

BOTTOMLY: Okay, what did you do then?

DESALVO: There was a coffee table to the right, and I propped her legs up, and I had intercourse with her.

BOTTOMLY: Did you get bloody?

DESALVO: No.

BOTTOMLY: She was very light. . . .

DESALVO: Yes, and she started to come to.

BOTTOMLY: She did?

DESALVO: Yes.

BOTTOMLY: And did you relieve yourself at any time with respect to the colored girl?

DESALVO: I . . . I came inside her.

BOTTOMLY: Did you come anywhere but inside her?

DESALVO: It's possible that I did come on the floor afterwards.

BOTTOMLY: And what did you do after you had intercourse with her?

DESALVO: Well, she started to wake up, and I grabbed a nylon stocking, and she was the one I had to tie really tightly. . . . She started to fight, and I know I made it so tight I was unable to see it.

BOTTOMLY: And what kind of knot did you put in the stocking?

DESALVO: Three and one . . . two turns over and one. One on top.

BOTTOMLY: Okay, so it's two.

DESALVO: And I also . . . when she was . . . well, that's another reason why that I put the panties in her mouth, because she's waking up, but she's still not able to do nothing. To keep her from screaming, I put her pants in her mouth.

BOTTOMLY: And what about the clothes that she was wearing as you walked in, and what was there at the last?

DESALVO: I stripped her naked. I stripped her naked, I do recall this.

BOTTOMLY: Was she wearing a bra?

DESALVO: Yes.

BOTTOMLY: Was she wearing anything else also?

DESALVO: There could have been a half-slip.

BOTTOMLY: Anything else?

DESALVO: A white . . . she had stockings on and shoes.

BOTTOMLY: Now, did you do anything else with the bra?

DESALVO: The bra I could have put around her neck, but I'm not sure on this one.

BOTTOMLY: Did you put anything else around her neck? Other than the bra and her stocking?

DESALVO: Yes . . . a kerchief . . . no, let me think. Let me think . . .

BOTTOMLY: Something she might be wearing?

DESALVO: Yes.

BOTTOMLY: What?

DESALVO: [A] blouse. Ah, this is a [snaps fingers] . . . let me think . . .

BOTTOMLY: Remember, now, she started to come to and you had to put the panties in her mouth, and you tied the very tight knot with the stocking . . .

DESALVO: Could be a handkerchief.

Professional law enforcement agents cite this passage as another example of how not to conduct an interrogation. DeSalvo claims he ejaculated inside Clark, but Bottomly then slyly indicates the killer also ejaculated elsewhere in the apartment. DeSalvo makes a mistake by saying he "stripped her naked." Knowing this is not true, Bottomly then asks him if he kept her bra on, in effect steering De-Salvo back onto the right track. When the interrogator asks DeSalvo if he "did anything else with the bra," the question implies that the killer used more than one ligature.

Even with Bottomly's none-too-subtle assistance, De-Salvo's efforts to implicate himself in the Clark murder were so flawed that they should have been repudiated by authorities. First, DeSalvo told Bottomly that Sophie Clark had greeted him at the front door without her glasses on. However, Clark's roommates said she had very poor eyesight and was never seen without her eye-glasses. DeSalvo also incorrectly described the color of Clark's bathrobe, telling Bottomly it was a "white-type throw-on." Clark had been wearing a blue floral house-coat when she was killed. In addition, DeSalvo claimed the victim had been wearing black high heels, but the case file indicates that at the time of her death she had on rubber-soled loafers. Finally, DeSalvo maintained he had seen several musical instruments and some bottles when he walked in the front door of the flat. There were no instruments or empty bottles inside Clark's apartment.

Admittedly, DeSalvo correctly stated that Sophie Clark had been menstruating, a fact never reported in the press. So where did he get his information? Jim Mellon claims that DeSalvo was coached by his lawyer and members of the Boston Strangler Task Force. After all, it was in their interest to make DeSalvo the Boston Strangler.

DeSalvo also could have received details of the killings from George Nassar, who himself was a suspect in the murder of Sophie Clark. At the time of her death, he lived just a few blocks away from her, in Boston's South End neighborhood. In his confession to Clark's murder, DeSalvo mentioned that he had visited the apartment of another black woman in Clark's building, at 315 Huntington Avenue, that same day. He said he had told the woman he was there to do some painting, but was scared off when the woman claimed her husband was next door and would be home soon. Marcella Lulka, a resident of 315 Huntington Avenue, told the police that a man had knocked on her door the day Clark was murdered. She described the man as approximately five feet, nine inches tall, about 150 pounds, with brown hair. When police took Lulka to Bridgewater State Hospital in an effort to identify DeSalvo, Lulka watched as a group of inmates ate dinner, DeSalvo among them. Lulka said that DeSalvo was not the man who had come calling but that the man next to DeSalvo looked very familiar. That man was George Nassar.

DeSalvo's account of the killing of the twenty-six-year-old aspiring opera singer Beverly Samans also conflicted with known facts. The Samans killing bore little resemblance to the other Boston Strangler murders in that the Cambridge woman was not only strangled but also butchered. Susan Kelly, in her 1995 book *The Boston Stranglers,* writes that Albert DeSalvo told authorities he stabbed Samans twice with a switchblade that he later discarded in a marsh. In reality, she had been stabbed seventeen times to the throat and left breast. The murder weapon—a paring knife, not a switchblade—was found in the kitchen sink.

Patricia Bissette had been strangled inside her Park Drive apartment, just beyond Fenway Park. DeSalvo incorrectly told Bottomly the woman lived across the street from a hospital. He also said he had taken her pajama bottoms off in the living room and then forced her to strip completely naked. Bissette's pajama bottoms were actually found in her bedroom, and she was not naked but wearing her bathrobe when police discovered her body.

DeSalvo's photographic memory also failed him when he was asked to describe the murder of strangler victim number nine, Evelyn Corbin. DeSalvo claimed he had talked his way into Corbin's apartment and then forced her to have sex. He said Corbin complained that because of a physical condition, she could not have intercourse but under duress, she offered to perform oral sex. But there is no mention in Corbin's autopsy report about a preexisting medical condition and the oral sex act had been described in the newspaper. DeSalvo added that after the sex assault, he had choked Corbin with his bare hands and then used a pair of nylons to finish the job. But Corbin's hyoid bone and the cartilages of her larynx and trachea were intact. DeSalvo described the victim as five foot, five inches tall with brown hair. Corbin was only five foot, two inches tall, and her hair was platinum blond. DeSalvo also described reddish wallpaper in her apartment, but Corbin's walls were stucco. Of the major details that DeSalvo did get right in the Corbin murder, most had been printed in the newspapers.

Despite DeSalvo's repeated mistakes, Bottomly pressed on. The tenth victim would be next, twenty-two-year-old Joann Graff. Although DeSalvo liked to visit the scenes of the strangler's crimes, he clearly never had traveled to Graff's apartment in Lawrence. DeSalvo told Bottomly that Graff lived on the first floor of her building; her apartment was on the third floor. He described it as a "one-room flat." He apartment had a separate kitchen and a bathroom. He said Graff had been wearing a black leotard when he strangled her. Every newspaper account mentioned that Graff had been strangled with a leotard, but because her slacks and panties were found intertwined on the bedroom floor, police believed it was unlikely that she had been wearing the leotard found around her neck. DeSalvo claimed he had strangled her with the leotard and a single nylon stocking, but the autopsy report states that two nylon stockings were tied around her throat. DeSalvo, the man described by psychiatrists as having a photograph memory, could not even remember the month of Graff's murder. He could remember only that it had occurred sometime after September 1963.

5 : The Home Front

It had been more than a year since Mary Sullivan's murder, and her sister Diane had lost all hope that police would find the killer. Diane had graduated from Barnstable High School, but instead of backpacking across Europe with her older sister as they had planned, she went to work as a hairdresser in her aunt's beauty salon. Though she maintained a cheery outlook on life to her friends and coworkers, there was pain inside.

She did find comfort with her boyfriend, Donny Sherman, an active-duty marine who had been introduced to her by Mary. In the months after the murder, Diane had felt a need to get on with her life and jumped at the chance to marry him soon after high school graduation. Following a small wedding, Donny went back to duty with the U.S. Marines, and Diane remained on Cape Cod, awaiting the birth of their first child and dreading the thought of the first anniversary of her sister's murder. On January 4, 1965, when she was nine months pregnant, Diane once again drove to Sea Street Beach to talk to her sister. Despite a strong winter chill coming off the water, a warm feeling came over Diane as she walked the snow-covered sand. She held her growing stomach and asked her angel Mary to watch over her baby. Two weeks later, on January 19, 1965, Diane gave birth to a son, Todd Forrest Sherman.

As Diane grew into her new and demanding role as a mother, she never lost sight of the Boston Strangler investigation. Because the family no longer received phone calls from the police, Diane had to rely on newspapers for updates on the search for Mary's killer. Yet the story, which had dominated the news for so long, now was relegated to an occasional mention. John Bottomly was keeping Albert DeSalvo's confessions a secret from everyone, including his own boss, Attorney General Edward Brooke, who was engaged in a tight race for the U.S. Senate, with his hope for success seemingly tied to a resolution of the Boston Strangler case. (Bottomly was concerned that Brooke would see the flaws in his interrogation of DeSalvo.) Brooke had promised the public swift justice when his office took over the case, and he believed the public would not forgive him if the killer or killers were not found soon.

An FBI memorandum dated September 24, 1965, states that its Boston office had received information from the Massachusetts attorney general's office and the Boston commissioner of police indicating that local authorities believed they had located the person responsible for the eleven strangulation murders that had occurred in Boston. Local authorities identified the suspect to the FBI as Albert Henry DeSalvo, then incarcerated at the Bridgewater State Hospital in Massachusetts.

Though the federal authorities were supplied with a

name, they weren't told much else. In a letter to James L. Handley, special agent in charge of the Boston office of the FBI dated October 29, 1965, John Bottomly wrote that "because of the present state of the investigations and the demands associated with the preparation of cases for possible presentation to grand juries, it does not appear to be appropriate at this time to divulge information about the modus operandi or possible admissions of Albert Henry DeSalvo. However, please be assured that this Department [the attorney general's office] will cooperate at the earliest possible date when disclosure of such information could not possibly jeopardize investigations or legal proceedings."

John Bottomly was apparently trying to buy time. If he gave DeSalvo's confession tapes to the FBI, serious questions could be raised about the man's guilt. DeSalvo himself did not share these worries. He was now completely immersed in his new role as the Boston Strangler, a designation that certainly carried more weight with his fellow inmates than the Measuring Man. DeSalvo even added two more names to the victims' list, sixty-nine-year-old Mary Brown and eighty-five-year-old Mary Mullen. As with his other confessions, DeSalvo did not let the facts stand in the way of a good story. Mary Brown had been stabbed to death on March 9, 1963, inside her Lawrence home. When asked to describe the place, DeSalvo said Brown lived in a gray clapboard house. The house was actually painted brown with asbestos shingling. DeSalvo also said that when he entered the home, he had had to open a door and turn right to go up the stairs. The stairs were in fact straight ahead from the door. DeSalvo then claimed that he had grabbed a fork from the silverware drawer and stabbed Brown in the right breast. Photos taken at the crime scene showed that Brown had been stabbed in the left breast. Finally, De-Salvo said he had not had time to steal anything from the apartment. But again, crime scene photos contradicted his confession. The victim's apartment had been ransacked.

Mary Mullen died nearly a year before Mary Brown. Albert DeSalvo remembered every detail in the Mullen case because he was there on the night she died. Mullen's death was not a homicide, however; she had dropped dead of a heart attack when she saw DeSalvo. He had told his brother Richard that he had broken into an elderly woman's apartment on Commonwealth Avenue in Boston on June 28, 1962, having thought no one was home and he would have plenty of time to search for valuables. But when he entered the apartment, he was startled to find Mary Mullen in her bathrobe in the hall-way. The fright was too much for Mullen, who collapsed on the floor. DeSalvo told his family that he had picked up the dead woman, placed her on the couch, and covered her body with a blanket. Mullen's death is the only one DeSalvo was really responsible for, and it tore him up in-side. Richard DeSalvo says Albert wept when he spoke about the experience and swore he would stop breaking into people's homes.

In the autumn of 1965, John Bottomly found himself at a crossroads. He knew he could never successfully prosecute DeSalvo for the Boston Strangler murders. First, there was not a shred of physical evidence against him. And because of his unusual agreement with F. Lee Bailey, Bottomly could not use DeSalvo's confessions in a court of law. This agreement turned out to be a blessing in disguise for Bottomly because once a jury was made aware of the major discrepancies between the confessions and the actual crime scenes, the state may well not have been able to gain a conviction.

So how do you convince the public a case is solved without ever securing a conviction in a court of law? The answer was to serve DeSalvo to the media as the Boston Strangler but to prosecute him as the Green Man. DeSalvo was eager to sign a book deal for his life story. F. Lee Bailey also wanted to hurry along the book project because that would give DeSalvo the money to pay Bailey. Bottomly set the plan in motion, but then he made a surprising report on April 8, 1966. He announced his resignation from the attorney general's office effective immediately, giving no reason for the departure. This was Bottomly's last chess move, and he played it well. By resigning, he might be spared any fallout the strangler case might have. Bottomly did not turn in the keys to his office until he made certain his successor would go along with the plan. In a confidential memo dated just six days after Bottomly's resignation, the successor, Herbert Travers, wrote to Attorney General Edward Brooke that "there is at present no admissible evidence that can be used to convict DeSalvo on any of the [now] 13 deaths. The District Attorney of Middlesex County however does have strong evidence against DeSalvo on a dozen or so lesser sex offenses." The stage was set: Albert DeSalvo would stand trial for four rapes he had committed as the Green Man, but not for the Boston Strangler murders. In May 1966, DeSalvo was paraded before the cameras and declared the prime suspect in the Boston Strangler case. Diane Sullivan Sherman was rocked by the news. "I couldn't believe it. I still don't," she says. "I remember thinking, 'Who is this guy? Look at how he straightens his hair and tie every time a camera is on him.' He wanted too much to be the Boston Strangler. Call it intuition, but I just knew in my heart that this creep didn't kill my sister."

Still, the newspapers took the bait. They were so eager to call DeSalvo the Boston Strangler that they failed to note the fact that DeSalvo had not been charged with any of the murders. DeSalvo the Strangler sold newspapers, while DeSalvo the Green Man did not.

In July 1966, a judge ruled that DeSalvo was competent to stand trial for the Green Man rapes. The highly anticipated trial began the following January. In his opening statement, F. Lee Bailey told the jury his client had committed the sex assaults. DeSalvo had done it, Bailey argued, because he was insane. What sane man, he asked, would rape four women and also strangle thirteen more? Bailey was trying to slip in evidence from the Boston Strangler case to bolster his position in the Green Man case. The prosecutor quickly objected but was overruled. Bailey also called several psychiatrists to testify that DeSalvo was insane. The first was Dr. James Brussel from the New York State Department of Mental Health. Brussel told jurors that DeSalvo was driven by overwhelming sexual urges that he could not curb. "He has created by means of a schizophrenic process a world of his own where he simply reigns supreme," Brussel maintained. Another psychiatrist, Dr. Robert Ross Mezer, told the jury that he, too, believed DeSalvo was a schizophrenic, insisting that although the defendant knew he was committing crimes, he did not have the capacity to conform to the requirements of the law.

When the state got its turn, the prosecutor, Donald L. Conn, surprised observers by putting an ex-convict on the stand. Stanley Setterlund, a former inmate, testified that he had met DeSalvo at Bridgewater State Hospital in January 1965. "He said he had something bigger than the Brink's robbery and the Plymouth mail robbery," Setterlund told the jury. When asked to elaborate, Setterlund testified that DeSalvo had spoken of murders that were worth a lot of money, $10,000 apiece. Setterlund also swore that DeSalvo boasted of magazine offers of more than $100,000 for his story and claimed there was talk of a movie deal worth a million.

In his closing argument, the prosecutor emphasized that Albert DeSalvo was not a sex maniac or a sick man but a cunning and clever manipulative criminal who should be sent to prison for life. And on January 18, 1967, DeSalvo was indeed convicted and sentenced to life in prison. In the public mind, the Boston Strangler was being punished for his crimes, and the case that had held the region in fear's grip for almost five years was finally over.

Diane Sullivan Sherman did not share this feeling. She was working at the beauty salon on the day of the verdict. Afterward, she drove to her in-laws' house to pick up her infant son, Todd. Diane still had a lot of cooking and cleaning to do in preparation for his first birthday party the next day. Her mother-in-law met her at the front door with the baby and a copy of the *Cape Cod Standard Times*, whose front page featured a headline story about DeSalvo's conviction. Diane crumpled up the newspaper and threw it in the trash. Then she picked up her baby and held him gently. "How can Mary rest with her killer still out there?" Diane wondered.

One other person shocked by the conviction was Albert DeSalvo. He had been promised that if he confessed to the murders, he would be sent to a state-of-the-art psychiatric hospital, one with fresh linens and decent food, where he could sit for hours with doctors, explaining to them what drove him mad. He would gain respect for being one of the most infamous criminals ever.

In fact, there would be no cushy hospital treatment. Middlesex County Superior Court Judge Cornelius J. Moynihan ordered DeSalvo to Walpole State Prison for the remainder of his natural life. The trip to the state penitentiary was put on hold, however, because Bailey appealed the sentence, at which point Moynihan suspended his order and DeSalvo was returned to Bridgewater. There DeSalvo and two other inmates, George Harrison and Frederick Erickson, launched a daring escape attempt in the frigid predawn hours of February 24, 1967. Erickson was serving a life sentence for murder after having stabbed his estranged wife to death. Harrison had been sentenced to fifteen years for armed robbery. The inmates planned the escape carefully. One of them stole a key to the cells, and all three stuffed their bedsheets to make it look as if they were still in bed sleeping. Then they crept down the corridor to where a new elevator was being installed. There they pried open the elevator door and climbed down the shaft to freedom. They were wearing prison clothing consisting of gray jackets and trousers, and DeSalvo reportedly was carrying an eight-shot .32 caliber Beretta, while the other two were armed with scissors.

When they got away from the hospital grounds, the escapees stole a car and drove to Boston, where DeSalvo dropped his fellow fugitives off at Haymarket Square in Boston's North End. DeSalvo knew he would have to change his appearance to avoid being recognized. His hooked nose was easily his most distinguishing feature, and he had told the others he was going to fly to Canada for a nose job. He would then kill the doctor who performed the operation and head to Mexico.

This was probably no more than a sensational story DeSalvo had concocted to impress the other men. In any case, by 6:20 A.M., it became known that the inmates were missing from their cells, and every police department in Massachusetts was notified. Meanwhile, panic spread among the citizenry. Women and children were told to stay in their houses. FBI dispatches were rolling off the teletype at the agency's branch offices in Ottawa, Canada, and Mexico City. Airports were checked, and flyers describing Albert DeSalvo were circulated throughout the country. The hunt for the so-called Boston Strangler was on.

A man fitting DeSalvo's description was spotted driving a white Ford four-door sedan in Washington, D.C., and DeSalvo was reportedly "seen" at a Greyhound Bus terminal in Richmond, Virginia, arguing with a clerk over a refund for a bus ticket. The *Boston Record American* offered a $5,000 reward for the strangler, dead or alive. In addition, the newspaper issued this warning: "Women Beware! He's a Cutie—Keep Chain Lock Bolted." Reached by the media in North Carolina, where he was working on a case, F. Lee Bailey said he'd double the *Record American* reward to $10,000, but only if his client was brought in alive.

Despite all the rumors, DeSalvo made it only forty miles from Bridgewater. After parting ways with Erickson and Harrison, he drove just north of Boston to Everett, where he met up with Joe, his older brother. Dumping the stolen car, he asked Joe to drop him off in

Lynn. By now it was getting late, and DeSalvo had nowhere to sleep. He did not know that his fellow fugitives were already under arrest, captured just thirteen hours after their escape while drinking beer at a bar in the town of Waltham.

DeSalvo knew he had to get off the streets before he was spotted. Cold, hungry, and tired, he broke into someone's cellar. He was still wearing the gray prisoner's uniform from the state hospital, but he rummaged through the cellar and found a Navy pea coat and bell-bottom trousers. He stayed hidden in the cellar until mid-morning the following day, when he strolled back into town, aiming to pass himself off as a sailor on leave, although he was not wearing the mandatory kerchief with his uniform blouse, and he had on brown dress shoes under his bell-bottoms.

In mid-afternoon, he walked into the Simon Uniform Store in Lynn, having decided to give himself up. The store owner and four salesmen were sitting around having coffee. "Can I use the phone?" DeSalvo asked sheepishly. "I want to call F. Lee."

None of the salesmen seemed afraid. "He knew [that] we knew who he was," the store owner told the Associated Press. "He wasn't a very big person, and he never went after men anyway."

After making his phone call, DeSalvo calmly stood by the water cooler and waited for police to arrive. The scene was serene inside the store, but word spread quickly, and two thousand people gathered outside the store to watch the notorious Boston Strangler surrender. "Kill him!" shouted some in the mob, which was growing more and more unruly. DeSalvo played to the crowd,

THE HOME FRONT 95

winking at some newsmen he recognized as he was ushered into a waiting squad car.

The judge remanded DeSalvo to the maximum-security
prison at Walpole. DeSalvo told reporters his escape was
not an attempt to get free and quench his blood thirst but
an effort to call attention to his need for rehabilitation.
"Maybe people will know what it means to be mentally
ill," he told reporters. F. Lee Bailey went even further
than his client had, suggesting to the press that the move
to Walpole State Prison could cause his troubled client to
commit suicide. Bailey swore to seek a writ of habeas
corpus to get DeSalvo sent back to Bridgewater. The request was denied. DeSalvo would spend the remainder of
his life behind the concrete walls of Walpole.

But all was not lost for DeSalvo. He made money from
Gerold Frank's book *The Boston Strangler,* having signed
over the rights to his life story. Frank never interviewed
DeSalvo; he got his information from F. Lee Bailey.
While Bailey says he never received a nickel from the
book, he did collect his attorney's fees from the DeSalvo
estate, and the only funds in the estate were proceeds
from the book, a best-seller and the basis of a movie. Jim
Mellon also spent several hours with Frank and was im-
pressed by the reporter's grasp of the complicated case.
"Finally, someone was going to tell the story right," Mellon said at the time, but his optimism did not last long. He
says, "I picked up the book, and couldn't get through the
first few pages, it was such bullshit." Mellon says he received a telephone call from Frank soon after the book
was published. "He asked me if I was upset by the book.
I said, 'Hell yeah! There's no way that DeSalvo is the
strangler.' He told me that I wasn't alone, and he apolo-

gized and blamed his rush to judgment on a strict publishing deadline."

The best-selling book was the beginning of what DeSalvo had hoped would become a lucrative business. He recorded a song entitled "Strangler in the Night" shortly after going to Walpole, and he set up a small business in the prison gift shop, selling choker necklaces with his name on them. He had other inmates do the work, and he collected the money. The necklaces still come up for sale on eBay from time to time.

The Boston Strangler case made F. Lee Bailey internationally famous. The day after DeSalvo's escape and subsequent capture, the *Washington Post* reporter Nicholas von Hoffman wrote a glowing article about Bailey that carried the headline "Bailey Plays Perry Mason in Case of Boston Strangler." Von Hoffman's article read like a Mickey Spillane novel. He described Bailey's office as an absolute mess, full of dirty ashtrays and empty whiskey bottles. "Even the brass replica of the scales of justice was out of balance. A throwback to Bogart," von Hoffman wrote. "I think the fun has just begun around here," Andrew Tuney, Bailey's investigator, told the reporter. "Wait till you see our new penthouse offices. And we're buying Frank Sinatra's Learjet for $400,000."

Von Hoffman reported that Tuney had gone to work as a private detective for Bailey after quitting his job with the Massachusetts State Police. The article did not mention that Tuney had been the lead investigator for the Boston Strangler Task Force.

6 : Lights, Camera, Action!

While F. Lee Bailey was shopping for Learjets and searching for his next high-profile client, Hollywood was beginning to take an interest in the Boston Strangler case. The Broadway producer Robert Fryer secured the film rights to *The Boston Strangler,* for which Albert DeSalvo did not receive a dime. By taking the option on the book, Fryer avoided buying the rights to DeSalvo's life story. But other key figures in the case were in a position to make big money. John Bottomly commanded the highest price. Twentieth Century Fox paid him $25,000, a sum that grew to $29,000 when Bottomly sold the life story rights of his wife and six children. According to Rick Davis, producer of the History Channel documentary "History through the Lens: The Boston Strangler: A Legacy of Terror," Edward Brooke, at the time a U.S. senator, received $20,000. Today Edward Brooke would be scrutinized for taking money while still in the senate, but back in the 1960s no one appeared concerned about this obvious conflict of interest. Meanwhile,

Mellon's former partner, Phil DiNatale, quit the Boston Police Department and took a job as a consultant on the film, for which he was paid $4,000, a lot of money in the 1960s. While DeSalvo got no money, the studio paid his wife $25,000 for the right to use the names of their children in the film.

Twentieth Century Fox chief Richard Zanuck assigned the director Richard Fleischer to make the movie and hired an Academy Award–winning writer, Edward Anhalt, to write the script. After reading the first drafts, F. Lee Bailey was angered that he would be only a minor character in the film, and he disassociated himself from the production. Fleischer wanted the movie to have a documentary feel and sought an unknown actor to play the DeSalvo role. More than two thousand men auditioned for the part. Unlike Fleischer, Twentieth Century Fox, which was putting $4 million into the production, wanted a big name to play the lead. Warren Beatty and Ryan O'Neal fought for the role. Other stars also auditioned, including Anthony Perkins, Peter Falk, and James Caan.

If he had to use a big star, Fleischer thought Tony Curtis was the perfect choice, but studio executives were aghast at the idea. Curtis, who had costarred in the Billy Wilder classic *Some Like It Hot,* was known for romantic comedy, not drama. But Fleischer was not to be denied. He told Curtis to morph himself into the notorious DeSalvo and pose for some pictures for the studio executives. Curtis put a wool stocking cap on his head, tilted it to one side, and smeared some putty on his nose to give himself more of a menacing look. Richard Zanuck loved what he saw, and Tony Curtis won the role.

Casting the role of John Bottomly was an easier task.

Henry Fonda said he committed to the movie after reading the last scene in the script. "The end of the picture, when the character of Bottomly faces *mano a mano* the DeSalvo character and finally breaks him down to the admission that he is the strangler, is a fascinating scene to play," Fonda said during a 1968 press junket to promote the film.

Production began on January 21, 1968, with most of the shooting on location in Boston. Diane Sullivan Sherman remembers walking by the Hyannis Theater and seeing the movie poster with Tony Curtis's fiendish eyes staring at her. The billboard read simply, "COME IN — HE DID 13 TIMES." Diane wondered whether she would have the strength or the desire to see her sister's murder enacted on the big screen.

The Boston Strangler opened on October 16, 1968, though DeSalvo had sued to block the film's New York premiere. No doubt he was angry that he had received no money and that the moviemakers never contacted him during the production. DeSalvo's filing claimed he was falsely depicted in the movie. A judge threw out the lawsuit, and *The Boston Strangler* opened to glowing reviews. Film critics raved about the performances of Tony Curtis and Henry Fonda. Some said the movie broke new cinematic ground with its use of split screen and multi-imaging, bringing the audience right into the chaos and terror of the events it depicted.

The film faced its harshest criticism from the men who had actually lived the events it depicted. "The movie showed John Bottomly rushing to the crime scenes. He'd never been to one murder scene," bristled Jim Mellon. The film twisted other facts. In one scene, Bottomly comes face to face with DeSalvo during a chance meeting at a mental hospital, notices a bite mark on DeSalvo's hand, and deduces that he's the Boston Strangler. In reality, F. Lee Bailey handed DeSalvo over to the authorities. DeSalvo never received a bite mark from any of his alleged victims.

Yet Hollywood convinced the world that Albert DeSalvo was the Boston Strangler. Granted, moviemakers had help from DeSalvo himself. But he was never tried for the murders in a court of law. Albert DeSalvo's only trial came on celluloid, and audiences around the world came away convinced that what they saw was true.

Along with the investigators, there was another nonbeliever in the film's audience: Mary's sister Diane, who had finally summoned the courage to go to the theater. Some theatergoers recognized Diane as a sister of a strangler victim, and whispers spread through the movie house. One hand gripped tightly around her husband's, the other hand clenching the side of her seat as the opening credits rolled, Diane vowed not to leave the theater no matter how bad it got. Fortunately, the filmmakers had changed the names of the victims, so Diane had no idea which scene showed her sister's murder. Still, she was angry with Tony Curtis. "I found it so disgusting," she recalls. "This big Hollywood star playing such a fraud! I thought to myself, 'DeSalvo must be loving this.'"

The Boston Strangler grossed $16 million at the box office, and there was even talk of an Oscar nomination for Tony Curtis. In the end, he didn't get the nomination, but some of those connected to the actual case were rewarded. Edward Brooke had won his race for U.S. senate. After serving as a technical adviser on the movie, Detective Phil DiNatale opened a private investigation firm in the Boston area. F. Lee Bailey set up Andy Tuney and a fellow task force alumnus, Stephen Delaney, in their own private investigation office. Others who had worked on the case rose quickly through the ranks of the Boston Police Department.

Meanwhile, DeSalvo's wife, Irmgard, filed for divorce and took the children back to her native Germany. DeSalvo had no money, no family, and no reason to continue his charade of being the Boston Strangler. The man who had caused widespread panic when he escaped from Bridgewater State Hospital now was relegated to dancing with elderly women on senior day at the prison. The only family member who did not cut ties with him was his younger brother, Richard. Richard and his wife, Rosalie, visited DeSalvo regularly at Walpole. It disturbed Richard that they never got to meet Albert alone; at Albert's insistence, there always was another inmate there during the visits. That inmate was George Nassar. After being found guilty of the murder of a gas station attendant, Irving Hilton, Nassar had also been sentenced to life in prison at Walpole.

During visits with his brother, Albert always tried to keep the conversation light. Richard recalls one particular visit when his brother told him he was not the Boston Strangler. "You wanna know who the real strangler is?" he asked with a grin. "He's right next to me," Albert said, nudging his buddy George. At that, Nassar's teeth clenched, and he shot a hard look at DeSalvo.

During a later visit by Richard, the usually jovial Albert appeared tense. He told Richard that something big was going to break and that he was getting ready to "blow the lid off this whole thing." He then warned his brother not to visit him at Walpole for a while. "Things are getting hot," he said. When the prison guard told DeSalvo he

102 Search for the Strangler

was out of time, he stood up and hugged his younger brother, not wanting to let go. "He had never done that before," Richard remembers. "I knew something bad was about to happen."

Richard DeSalvo was not the only person Albert confided in. He also called the psychiatrist Ames Robey. Robey says, "I got a call from Albert, and he said, 'I want you to come to Walpole tomorrow. I have a reporter who's going to meet with me, and I want to tell the real story.'" Robey had not heard from DeSalvo for several years and was surprised by the telephone call. But he was also curious, and he told DeSalvo he would be there for the meeting.

The next morning, November 26, 1973, after Robey got into his car and began the drive to Walpole, he turned on the radio and heard the news: the Boston Strangler had been found stabbed to death in prison. Robey almost drove off the road. What he did not know was that DeSalvo, afraid for his life, had put himself in the infirmary, the most secure section of the prison. Inmates had to clear six security checkpoints to get in and out of the infirmary. Yet the killer got through all six checkpoints, stabbed DeSalvo repeatedly in the heart, and went back through security covered in blood, and no one indicated having seen a thing. It was an execution, pure and simple. Some say DeSalvo was murdered because of a squabble over a few pounds of bacon. Others, including F. Lee Bailey, claim DeSalvo was heavily involved in the prison narcotics trade and paid the price for trying to undercut fellow drug dealers. Still others swear DeSalvo was murdered to keep him from talking about the Boston Strangler case. Some of these, former inmates, claim it was a contract hit: the killer was said to have been paid $50,000 by someone from the outside. The person who paid, the inmates say, was the one who had the most to lose if DeSalvo told the true story. DeSalvo's killer was rumored to be Vincent "The Bear" Flemmi, a ruthless Mafia hit man who later died in prison of a heroin overdose. Three other inmates were eventually charged and tried twice for Albert De-Salvo's murder; both trials ended in hung juries. But De-Salvo would continue to pique the public's curiosity from the grave. A poem he wrote was discovered shortly after his murder.

Here is the story of the Strangler, yet untold.
The man who claims he killed thirteen women, young
    and old.
The elusive Strangler, there he goes.
Where his wanderlust sends him, no one knows.
He struck within the light of day.
Leaving not one clue astray.
Young and old, their lips are sealed.
Their secret of death never revealed.
Even though he is sick in mind,
He's much too clever for the police to find.
To reveal his secret will bring him fame,
But burden his family with unwanted shame.
Today he sits in a prison cell,
Deep inside only a secret he can tell.
People everywhere are still in doubt,
Is the Strangler in prison, or roaming about?

7 : All the King's Men

In the years following the murder of Albert DeSalvo, key figures in the Boston Strangler case were plagued by a series of scandals, beginning with John Bottomly. The real estate attorney had gone back into private practice soon after the Boston Strangler movie was released in 1968. That same year, he "discovered" that bearer bonds worth $60,000 were missing from his law office. The bonds were part of a trust that Bottomly was overseeing. When beneficiaries pressed Bottomly about the status of the trust, he answered evasively, never explaining that their money was missing. Finally, they hired a lawyer to go after Bottomly. The missing funds were never recovered, but Bottomly and his wife ended up paying $150,000 to cover the bonds, interest, and related taxes and penalties. When the case finally reached the Massachusetts Superior Court in 1980, Judge Paul J. Liacos suspended Bottomly from practicing law in Massachusetts. Bottomly's troubles did not cease there, either. In 1981 he pleaded guilty to charges that he had failed to pay his taxes from 1974 to 1977. Bottomly left Massachusetts in disgrace, moving his family to Salt Lake City.

When he died of a heart attack at age sixty-three, during a return visit to Massachusetts in August 1984, John Bottomly left many unanswered questions about his role in the Boston Strangler case. Probably the most important concerns the confession of Albert DeSalvo. Bottomly, who tape-recorded sixty hours of conversations with DeSalvo in 1965, claimed he placed the tapes in a bank vault shortly thereafter. The original tapes have never been found.

Edward Brooke's reputation would also be tarnished. He lost his bid for reelection against Democrat Paul Tsongas in 1978, after revelations that Brooke had lied under oath about his financial situation while being deposed for his divorce. Brooke's legal adviser at the time was his old friend John Bottomly. Edward Brooke would never again be a power player in Massachusetts politics.

F. Lee Bailey would also fall from grace. He had been fired by DeSalvo in 1968 over the movie deal with Twentieth Century Fox. Business, however, had never been better. Bailey opened two more law offices, one in New York, the other in Florida. He had a helicopter pad built on his property in Marshfield, along the South Shore of Massachusetts, so that instead of having to abide a twenty-five minute commute to Boston, the flamboyant attorney could fly to and from the office. Bailey's next big case after DeSalvo was defending the newspaper heiress Patty Hearst against charges that she had robbed a San Francisco bank in 1974 with members of a radical group called the Symbionese Liberation Army. Hearst, who had been caught on a bank surveillance camera wielding a machine gun during the holdup, claimed the radicals had kidnapped her from her Berkeley, California, home and forced her to participate in the robbery. The Patty Hearst case made headlines around the world. It was fitting that the beautiful granddaughter of the king of yellow journalism, William Randolph Hearst, would become fodder for tabloids and the mainstream press.

During the Hearst trial, Bailey made the disastrous decision to put Hearst on the witness stand, where she exercised her Fifth Amendment rights forty-two times. Hearst was quickly convicted of armed robbery and sentenced to seven years in prison. What the young heiress did not know at the time, however, was that her attorney had signed a lucrative book deal during the trial. Hearst, whose sentence was later commuted by President Jimmy Carter, used Bailey's alleged conflict of interest in a bid to overturn her robbery conviction.

In October 1980, the Ninth U.S. Circuit Court of Appeals ruled that there were "serious questions" concerning whether Bailey and his cocounsel, J. Albert Johnson, were guilty of conduct unbecoming members of the bar. "Bailey's potential conflict of interest is virtually admitted," the court declared. Despite the serious questions raised, Hearst's bid to overturn her conviction would eventually be denied. Nevertheless, the luster was beginning to fade on Bailey's reputation.

Soon his problems would get worse. In 1982, Bailey was arrested in San Francisco for drunk driving after being pulled over in a borrowed Mercedes-Benz after running a stop sign. The arresting officers said they had been forced to slap handcuffs on Bailey after he became belligerent. San Francisco police sergeant Lawrence McKenzie, who participated in the arrest, said Bailey was "very arrogant and pompous and extremely obnoxious to everybody in the immediate vicinity."

At the police station, Bailey refused to take a sobriety test and would not sign a property sheet for his belongings or sign for his allowed telephone call. The prosecution called thirty witnesses at Bailey's trial in April. Each testified that Bailey had acted peculiarly and irrationally. Bailey's attorney, Robert Shapiro, had one ace in the hole, however: a lack of concrete evidence that his client was drunk at the time of his arrest. It was good enough to gain an acquittal. Nonetheless, the California Department of Motor Vehicles suspended Bailey's driver's license for six months because of his refusal to take the sobriety test.

A year later, Massachusetts made public the names of more than a thousand of the worst tax evaders in the state. One name on the list was that of F. Lee Bailey, who owed $57,562 in back taxes. In response to this news, Massachusetts Governor Michael Dukakis asked the state legislature to suspend Bailey's license to practice law, but lawmakers never took action against Bailey. The default eventually was settled, and Bailey would remain out of the public eye until the "trial of the century" a decade later, the murder trial of football legend O. J. Simpson.

8 : The Portrait on the Mantel

The Sullivan family sought to move beyond Mary's murder. Their home on Sea Street in Hyannis, once filled with Mary's cheerful voice, was now ringing with the sounds of grandchildren. As Diane's second son, born on January 19, 1969, I was part of the baby boom in the Sullivan family. My earliest memories of my grandparents' house are joy-filled. It was always the setting for large family gatherings during the holidays. My brother, Todd, our cousins, and I would spend hours exploring the old house, finding new spots to hide. Our favorite place was in a spare bedroom just above the kitchen. A small vent in the bedroom allowed us to listen to the conversations the grown-ups were having on the floor below. Their talk usually bored us, though. They'd discuss the news of the day, work, and us kids.

One topic that apparently was off limits was my Aunt Mary's death. I knew Aunt Mary only from her portrait on the mantelpiece, the same picture that had fallen and whose frame had been smashed after her funeral. Her reframed portrait stood among those of other family members. I would stare at the photo often as a child, mesmerized by Mary's chestnut hair, brown eyes, and the sober look on her face. She appeared very sad to me. My mother, for her part, was not fond of the picture. "I prefer to remember her smiling," she would say. Still, Mom never told me what had happened to her sister. An inquisitive little boy, I would always ask her who the sad lady in the picture was. "She was my sister and my best friend," Mom would reply. "Where is she?" I'd ask. "When you're older," she would say and kiss my cheek. "When you're older."

Years passed. During the summer of 1988, before I entered college, I was sitting on the couch at home with the remote control in hand, flipping through television channels, when I came across the movie *The Boston Strangler* on Channel 38. I sat glued to the television set watching Tony Curtis go from apartment to apartment, offering women his killer smile and then something even more deadly. "So this is how it happened," I thought.

The next day, I felt uncomfortable, not knowing how to broach the subject with my mother. She had already experienced enough pain in her life. My mother's third child had been stillborn, and we were both grieving the loss of my father, Donny Sherman, who had died suddenly in 1986. Over breakfast, we chatted about my summer job and even the pitching rotation of the Red Sox. Finally, I got up the nerve. "Mom," I said, "tell me what happened to Mary." She put her cup of coffee down on the kitchen counter. "I remember the last time I saw her. It was Christmas," she recalled. "We were having such a great time. I remember twice saying, to her, 'Mary, why move up to Boston now? Stay another week. We're having so much fun.' I always wonder if she would have stayed if I asked her one more time." Mom spent the next several minutes telling me about Mary's murder. I could hear the pain in her voice. Trying to console her, I walked over to her chair and placed an arm on her shoulder. "At least they got the guy," I said. Mom looked up at me sadly. "No, no, they never did," she replied.

My mother's words gave me my life's mission. I wanted to ease her pain, but how? I did not see myself becoming a police officer. Calling me undersized would be an understatement. At five foot, two inches, there was no way I could meet the law enforcement height requirement. So I decided to become a journalist. I realized that a pen and notepad could be just as effective as a gun and badge when it came to getting to the truth.

At first, I wanted to prove that my mother was wrong and that Albert DeSalvo really was who he claimed to be. By doing so, I might close this heart-wrenching chapter in Mom's life. I knew that DeSalvo had been murdered in prison and if we were certain he was Mary's killer, we could gain a certain sense of Old Testament justice from that.

As a journalism student at Boston University, I sat through countless lectures on story structure, lead writing, and interviewing. I showed an aptitude for the work and was an above-average student for the first time in my life. But my real training as a reporter would come at night in the bowels of the college library. Fortunately, the library had microfiche copies of all the local papers, dating back several decades. I grabbed a film reel labeled "*The Boston Globe*" dated 1964, fastened it to the machine, and started to read, scrolling up to January 5, the day after Mary had been killed. My aunt's face staring up at me from the monitor, I read the news story, which made heavy use of the words *strangled, murder,* and *rape.* Suddenly I got up and ran to the nearest bathroom, where I lost my dinner. Mary's murder had become real to me for the first time.

I went back to the microfiche collection and kept returning there, night after night. The more I read, the more questions I developed about the case. Each newspaper story contradicted the one that had preceded it. Some reporters had left out key facts, while others had obviously created facts in an effort to tell a more sensational story. In short, newspapers were useless. To learn the truth, I would have to track down the people who had actually worked on the case. In the autumn of 1991, I went to a professor in the broadcast journalism department at the university and pitched the idea of doing a class project on the Boston Strangler case. "What is there left to tell?" the professor asked. "Everything," I answered. She told me to go ahead and see what I could find out.

The first person I called was Tom Troy, the Boston attorney Albert DeSalvo hired after firing F. Lee Bailey. Troy represented DeSalvo in his unsuccessful attempt to block the opening of *The Boston Strangler.* The six-foot, two-hundred-pound Troy rivaled Bailey for flamboyance. If Bailey had the private plane, Tom Troy often rented helicopters to make grand entrances in front of courthouses all over Massachusetts. Troy was the son of a Boston cop shot dead in the line of duty two weeks after Troy was born. His mother had to raise a family that included his brother and two sisters on a $35,000 trust fund established by a local newspaper. Troy argued his first case in front of a judge when he was just fifteen years old, saying that his father's killer should not be paroled. The killer's parole was denied. Troy was best known for defending a Tufts University professor, William Douglas, who had been charged with the murder of a Boston prostitute, Robin Benedict. Although no body was ever found, Douglas confessed to the killing just before his trial was about to begin.

Needless to say, Troy had no reason to sit down for an interview with a college lad. "Look, kid, I'm heading down to Florida this afternoon and don't have time for this stuff. Why are you interested in the story anyway?" he asked me. I told him who my aunt was and that I was beginning to doubt that Albert DeSalvo was the killer. "Casey," Troy replied, "I'm sorry to hear about your aunt, I really am. Let me tell you something about Silky DeSalvo. He was no more the strangler than you or me." "What makes you so certain?" I asked. He said, "First of all, the guy didn't have a violent bone in his body. He was a lover, not a killer. And besides, he told me that the story was bullshit." I wanted clarification. "You mean he told you that he wasn't the strangler?" I asked. "That's right," Troy replied. "Albert DeSalvo told me that he was not the Boston Strangler."

The next name on my list was Dr. Ames Robey. The psychiatrist agreed to meet me on the BU campus. This time, I wanted to make sure I got the interview on tape. I negotiated with a classmate, offering to shoot his video project in return for use of his camera. The deal was struck just as Robey was making his way up the steps of the College of Communications. A large man, Robey cut an impressive figure, even in his seventies. After telling me he still saw patients regularly in his Stoneham home, Robey discussed with me DeSalvo's psychological makeup, explaining that DeSalvo was not violent but prone to great exaggeration. Robey added that he thought George Nassar could have committed some of the Boston Strangler murders. "After so many years, is there any way this case can finally be solved?" I asked. Robey ran his hand over his bald head. "I know there was semen left at some of the crime scenes. With what's now being done with DNA testing, I don't see why not," he replied. DNA testing, I thought. Could it be the key that would unlock the case?

After the Robey interview, I went out to get footage of the outside of two of the apartment buildings where the women had been killed. With my borrowed video camera, I jumped on the subway, or the T, as it is called by Bostonians, and headed west on the Green Line, toward 1940 Commonwealth Avenue, the address of the Boston Strangler victim Nina Nichols.

It was a busy Friday afternoon in that part of the city. Many neighborhood residents were college students getting an early jump on the weekend. While I was setting up my shot, a few guys entered the building with cases of Budweiser under their arms. I hoped no one would walk into the middle of my shot. As several young women made their way in and out of the building, I wondered if they had any idea of what had taken place inside.

The last location on my shooting schedule was 44A Charles Street, an address I was in no rush to see. When I found my aunt's apartment building, I was unnerved by the fact that it looked exactly as it had in news photos from 1964. For a few moments I let my imagination get the better of me, traveling back in time to the day of Mary's murder. If I had been in my spot outside the building that day, would I have seen my aunt's killer as he entered her building? Could I have stopped him from committing the crime? I was brought back to reality when what had been a light drizzle turned to a heavy rain. Quickly videotaping several exterior shots of the building, I then walked a couple of blocks and ducked into a small tavern called The Sevens. Two men in suits were sitting at the bar, and a couple of construction workers were in the middle of a heated game of darts. "Brown-Eyed Girl" by Van Morrison played on the jukebox. The bar seemed familiar to me, almost as if I'd been there before. What I didn't know then was that The Sevens had been Mary's favorite pub during her brief stay in Boston. Sitting down at the mahogany bar, I ordered a beer and got lost in my thoughts. If only someone had seen something, I told myself. At that moment, I began to understand the questions and guilt my mother had been haunted by for so many years.

My obsession with the Boston Strangler case started to affect my love life. I didn't see or talk to my girlfriend for days. Laura Russell was an Irish-American lass, a finance major at Northeastern University with an adorable smile and a sharp mind. When we finally got together, she told me she had been noticing a change in me. Even when we were discussing our hopes for the future, my mind was somewhere in the past. Fortunately for me, Laura refused to let my involvement with the case drive a wedge between us. "It's really important to you, so it's important to me. If the only way to be with you is to become involved in this . . . I will," she told me one night, over pizza and beer at her apartment. And Laura turned out to be true to her word. She became my videographer.

My final interview subject was my mother. I wanted her to tell the world what she had been telling me, that Mary's killer could still be out there someplace. We shot the interview outside one sun-splashed autumn afternoon on the Boston Common. I gave Laura a crash course on filming and sat Mom down on a wooden bench for the interview. Making sure Laura was rolling tape, I asked my first question: "Mom, how does it feel being here in Boston, just blocks from the place where Mary was murdered?" My mother paused for a moment, searching her mind for the answer. "I don't want Mary to be just another statistic, victim number eleven," Mom said. "She was a real person, a beautiful girl and a loving sister."

Laura had never heard my Mom open up like that. "I can't believe she's carried this around for so long," Laura would say later. "Now I really know why you want to solve this case."

9 : Laying the Groundwork

After graduating from college, I began the job hunt. No Boston television stations were hiring reporters straight out of college, so I jumped from one low-level sales job to another. Frustrated, I would call my Nana Florry for a few words of encouragement. My grandmother and I were particularly close. She had watched my transformation from aimless teenager to driven adult. "You're better than anyone I've seen on TV," she said, trying to boost my confidence. By coincidence, the day I landed my first television job was the day Florry Sullivan died. I delivered the eulogy at her funeral. It was the spring of 1994, thirty years after Mary's murder. The Sullivan family had gathered once again at St. Francis Xavier Church to say good-bye.

The day after the funeral, I began work at WHDH Channel 7, which was then the CBS affiliate station in Boston. My first job was organizing scripts for the news anchors and running the teleprompter, for six dollars per hour. It did not matter to me that my friends were making

$20,000 and more in their first year out of college. Television news was where I wanted to be. I was drawn to its frantic atmosphere. There were deadlines for each of the daily newscasts, and they had to be met: your job depended on it. Assignment editors barked orders over the two-way radio to news crews out in the field. Producers pounded on their typewriters, quickly absorbing news stories as they came in, then sending them out as coherent scripts. As a production assistant, I ran script to the studio, most times just before the previous story was read. I would have considered myself lucky if anybody at the station even knew my first name.

Soon I was growing more concerned with my work at the station and less concerned with the Boston Strangler case. Then, in the fall of 1994, the name of Albert De-Salvo was suddenly in the news again. That's when Sean M. DeSalvo, his twenty-seven-year-old nephew, was arrested for the kidnapping and attempted rape of a forty-three-year-old Lynn woman. Of course, the newsroom had a field day. The file tapes of Albert DeSalvo and the Boston Strangler crime scenes were taken out of storage. "Imagine if we had another Boston Strangler. Now, that would be good for ratings," one veteran reporter said. I just bit my lip, hoping this story would go away and the references to the Boston Strangler case with it. However, the case of Sean DeSalvo would drag on for months and get even more bizarre. "He has tried to strangle me in my sleep," his wife, Claudia, claimed when she filed for divorce. "He has slept with a butcher knife under the pillow and told me he would not strangle me. If he killed me, he would stab me to death. I live in fear that my son could grow up to be the next Boston Strangler." How much of what she claimed was accurate and how much was rhet-

oric is unknown. However, kidnapping and attempted
rape charges against Sean DeSalvo were eventually
thrown out because of lack of evidence.

I was promoted to a newswriting position just as the
Trial of the Century was getting under way in Los Angeles. The legendary football player O. J. Simpson faced a
double murder charge for butchering his ex-wife, Nichole
Brown Simpson, and her friend Ron Goldman. Representing Simpson was the so-called Dream Team of
lawyers. The biggest name on the team was F. Lee Bailey. When the trial began, I was surprised to see the flamboyant and camera-conscious Bailey take a backseat to
two legal eagles of a new generation, Johnnie Cochran
and Barry Scheck. The trial was to rely heavily on scientific evidence and this was not Bailey's strong suit. The
prosecution team of Marcia Clark and Christopher Dar-
den had a mountain of evidence incriminating Simpson,
but evidence was no match for emotion. African Americans in Los Angeles were still seething from the Rodney
King beating, and Simpson's lawyers recognized that
many blacks distrusted the Los Angeles Police Department. There was a change in strategy and the Dream
Team elected to play the race card and place F. Lee Bailey
on center stage. It was Bailey who painted LAPD detective Mark Fuhrman as a racist because of the investigator's use of the word *nigger* in a taped interview.

Allowing Bailey to conduct Fuhrman's cross-examination was a bold move by the defense, considering that
Bailey himself had been chastised for using the same
word to describe Supreme Court Justice Thurgood Marshall during a speech in the 1970s. Bailey claimed he had
only spoken in fun that time. Anyway, Bailey was back
on top with his solid performance in the O. J. Simpson

Above left: Mary and Diane on the day of Diane's First Communion. The two sisters grew to be best friends. (Courtesy of Diane F. Dodd) *Above right:* Mary and her boyfriend Nathan Ward attending her senior prom at Barnstable High School in 1962. (Courtesy of Diane F. Dodd) *Left:* The portrait on the mantel. This photo both haunted and intrigued me when I was a child. (Courtesy of Diane F. Dodd)

Above: Charles Street as it looks today. The four-story building at left center is 44A (Photo by Casey Sherman) *Opposite above:* A crowd gathers in front of Mary's apartment building on January 4, 1964, after word spreads that the Boston Strangler has struck again. (Courtesy of the *Boston Herald*) *Opposite below:* Boston police carry Mary Sullivan's body out of 44A Charles Street. (Courtesy of the *Boston Herald*)

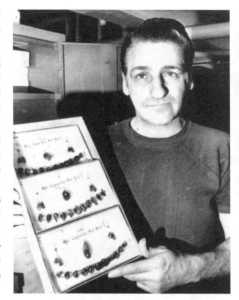

Right: Albert DeSalvo, the self-confessed Boston Strangler, posing with the necklaces he sold in the gift shop at Walpole State Prison. (Courtesy of the *Boston Herald*)

Below: George Nassar, the man many believe was one of the real Boston Stranglers. (UPI photo, courtesy of the *Boston Herald*)

Left: F. Lee Bailey, the charismatic young lawyer who was first brought into the Boston Strangler case to help broker a book deal for his client Albert DeSalvo. (Courtesy of the *Boston Herald*)

Below: Massachusetts Attorney General Edward Brooke briefs reporters on the Boston Strangler Task Force in August 1964. (UPI photo, courtesy of the *Boston Herald*)

Above: John Bottomly, the former real estate lawyer brought in to lead the Boston Strangler Task Force. (Courtesy of the *Boston Herald*) *Opposite above:* James Mellon, an original member of the Boston Strangler Task Force, who has never believed Albert DeSalvo was the real killer. (Photo by Casey Sherman) *Opposite below:* Michael DeSalvo, the only son of Albert and a living victim of the Boston Strangler Case. (Courtesy of WBZ-TV)

Above: The author confers with Jim Starrs at St. Francis Xavier Cemetery in Centerville, Massachusetts. (Photo by Elaine Whitfield Sharp) *Below:* Diane Sullivan Dodd thanks Jim Starrs for volunteering on the case. (Photo by Gaeton Cotton, Cottonphoto.com) *Opposite above:* Elaine Whitfield Sharp speaking at the first news conference (left to right: Diane Sullivan Dodd, James Starrs, Casey Sherman, Dr. David Benjamin, Elaine Sharp, Dan Sharp, Richard DeSalvo, Tim DeSalvo). (Photo by Gaeton Cotton, Cottonphoto.com) *Opposite below:* Professor James Starrs (center) oversees the exhumation of Mary Sullivan's remains. (Photo by Gaeton Cotton, Cottonphoto.com)

Left: Massachusetts Attorney General Tom Reilly. (Courtesy of the *Boston Herald*)

Below: Bartering for blood: Richard DeSalvo answers the challenge by taking a DNA test. (Courtesy of the *Boston Herald*)

case. But his triumph in that case was his last great victory before his downfall a few years later.

The O. J. Simpson trial was still the hottest news story when I left WHDH for an associate producer job at WTNH in New Haven, Connecticut. I needed to learn the details of news producing at a small station before I could jump to a producer job in Boston, the country's sixth largest media market. In New Haven I was quickly promoted to morning producer but had second thoughts when I realized the extent of my responsibilities. Producers not only choose which stories will be covered in a newscast; they also do the bulk of the writing and design the overall format of the show. But the biggest challenge facing most producers is dealing with the fragile egos of the on-air talent. Many anchor teams are not as chummy as they appear on-screen, and because news is so competitive, some coanchors will do just about anything to put down their on-air partners and get more time on-screen. It's the producer's job to divide the news fairly. I thought seriously about leaving television news, but where else would I find the forum to expose the inept investigation of the Boston Strangler case and identify Mary's killer? Television has long been our most powerful medium of communication. Newspaper stories lack the raw emotion conveyed by a good TV news story. But it takes a strong photographer, reporter, and producer to bring a television news story to life. I wanted to get back to Boston so I could work on the case, and I wanted to get back to spending time with Laura. Our relationship had grown stronger, but the three-hour commute from Boston to New Haven was exhausting for both of us. After asking her to marry me, I began calling television stations in Boston in hopes of finding work. I soon learned of a pro-

ducer opening at WBZ-4, Boston's oldest TV news station. During my interview, I told the news director I was
a student of the city's rich history and that to understand
Boston's future, you had to understand its past. The news
director, Peter Brown, apparently appreciated my approach and hired me. It was December 1996.

Brown was a very demanding boss. With live TV, anything can go wrong, and much does. If a reporter does not
make deadline or a live shot suddenly disappears because
of a technical difficulty, the producer must find a way to
get the show back on track.

And not only did Peter Brown insist that his producers
keep a clear head in the control booth, he also counted on
us to generate good story ideas. Story ideas usually are
discussed around a large conference table, with every
producer in attendance. At first, I did not tell anyone
about my connection to the biggest murder case in
Boston history. Instead, I waited for the right moment.
During a story meeting in the winter of 1997, Brown
went around the room asking each producer to come up
with three story ideas. Some suggestions were interesting, others had been done previously in other television
markets. Finally, all eyes rested on me. I was the new
guy, and I had better have something good. I took a deep
breath and told my story. My aunt had been the last victim in the Boston Strangler case, and I wanted to prove
that Albert DeSalvo was not the killer. The room fell
quiet. "Will your family talk on camera?" Peter Brown
asked finally. He knew a great story idea when he heard
it. "Absolutely," I told him.

10 : The Living Victims

When I got home that evening, I called my mother and explained my story idea. "You know, it's funny," she said. "I drove by Mary's grave today. I never go there because I hate to think of her in that cold ground. But there I was, talking to her headstone. I had this strong feeling come over me. It was Mary urging me to find her killer. It's time for everyone to know the truth." My mother would be the first relative of a Boston Strangler victim ever to go public with doubts about the guilt of Albert DeSalvo.

I wondered whether DeSalvo's family also had questions about his guilt. I scoured the telephone directory, hoping to find a DeSalvo relative still living in New England. I came across the name Frank DeSalvo in Revere. When I called, Frank DeSalvo confirmed that he was Albert's brother, but he also made it abundantly clear that he wanted nothing to do with a reinvestigation of the Boston Strangler case. "Why dig all that up again?" he asked. I explained there was a good chance we could prove that Albert was not the Boston Strangler, but he just replied, "Ah, who cares anymore?" At that point I realized there was no way to convince him to be interviewed for television.

After striking out with Frank, I found another of Albert's brothers, Richard, living in the town of Chelmsford. "Good afternoon, Richard, my name is Casey Sherman and I'm a producer at Channel 4 News in Boston," I said when I got him on the phone. There was a momentary silence at the other end of the line. As I later found out, this wasn't the first time a journalist had called Richard at home. "What can I do for you?" he finally asked. I said, "Well, sir, you and I have something in common. Your brother claimed to be the Boston Strangler, and my aunt was reportedly his last victim. But I don't believe it, and I'd like your help in proving it." "I never believed he was the strangler either," Richard said. I could tell by his voice that he was somewhat more at ease now. I went on to describe the story I was working on. "This is a story about the living victims of the Boston Strangler case. My mother is one . . . you, Richard, are another." In the end, Richard DeSalvo invited me to his home, though without committing to an on-camera interview.

I told my mother about the call to Richard. "Are you sure it's a good idea?" she asked. "I hate Albert DeSalvo. Every time I hear his name, I feel sick. If it wasn't for him, Mary's killer would have been found," Mom said. I reminded her that we should not hold DeSalvo's relatives responsible for his behavior. "They've felt years of pain, too," I pointed out.

On a blustery New England day in early March 1997, I drove to Chelmsford to talk to Richard DeSalvo. I believed that Albert DeSalvo was not a killer, but he was clearly a sexual predator. What would his family be like? Like him?

Despite my poor navigational skills, I managed to find

Richard DeSalvo's home, a small house in the middle of what appeared to be a massive renovation project. I climbed the front steps and knocked. Richard's wife, Rosalie, a small woman about the size of my mother, opened the door and showed me in. Richard was seated at the kitchen table. He did not get up to greet me; in fact, when I came in, he was looking away. But he held out his hand, and I took it. He had the strong grip of a man who worked with his hands. "Sorry, Casey, I don't see too good," he said. "He's actually legally blind," Rosalie added. Still shaking his hand, I gazed directly into his eyes. I had seen the look he wore many times before. My mother had the same look. It was the look of exhaustion, betrayal, and utter hopelessness. Also seated at the table was Richard's son, Tim, who eyed me a bit suspiciously.

"Listen, I'm sorry about your aunt," Richard began. "This has been hell for us, too. Police have been harassing me for years because of my brother. And now it's happening with my kids." Richard pointed across the table to his son. "He owns a construction company. The state police pulled him over a little while ago just because the name De-Salvo Construction was printed on the side of his truck," Richard said. Tim DeSalvo nodded in agreement.

I asked Richard why his brother had confessed to the murders. "The first time he was arrested and thrown in jail, he hated it," said Richard. "They wouldn't give him any clothes, barely nothin' to eat. My brother did not want to go to prison. F. Lee Bailey told him that if he confessed, he'd be put in a nice comfy hospital. Bailey also told Al he'd make so much money from books and movies that he'd own the hospital," Richard added, his voice growing louder as the anger welled up inside him. "But Al got nothing, and Bailey got everything. If it hadn't been for Bailey, my brother would be alive right now. I loved him. He may have done some stupid things, but he was still my brother."

I asked Richard whether Albert had ever told him he was not the Boston Strangler. Richard nodded. "Yes, he did. But I don't know how telling my story on TV could change things. I've told reporters for years that Al wasn't the guy, but they don't listen. They just write what they want to write," Richard said, pounding the table with his fist. Rosalie walked up behind him and began rubbing his back for comfort.

"I feel the same frustration you do, Richard," I said. "The reporters who covered this case never did their homework; if they did, we wouldn't be in this position right now. The public should know the pain you've gone through because it just isn't fair. In a way, you've been given a life sentence of your own."

Richard shook his head and said, "It's just too late for that, so I'm gonna have to say no." But I kept trying. "It's never too late for the truth," I said. "If you ever change your mind, you know where to find me."

"How many more people out there are still feeling pain over this?" I wondered as I got in my car and drove away.

Even without Richard's cooperation, WBZ aired a story anyway, focusing on my mother's interview and her long search for justice. Now it was time to find out if the Boston Police Department (BPD) was interested in taking another look at the case. I worked the newsroom telephones, focusing on the cold case squad at the BPD. I left numerous voice messages, but no one called back. Finally, after several days, I got through to one of the detectives. Introducing myself, I reminded him that since no one had ever been charged with my aunt's murder, her case remained open. The detective acknowledged that there were stories floating around that DeSalvo had not been the Boston Strangler. "But there's no new evidence to follow up on," he told me. I said, "You don't need new evidence. If you conduct DNA testing on the old evidence, it will prove that Albert DeSalvo wasn't the killer and that the real killers are still out there." The detective promised to get back to me, but he never did.

For a time then I focused on my upcoming wedding and my day-to-day work as a news producer. Laura and I were married in August 1997, around the time that we realized our other dream, which was to buy a house outside the city. I now had a loving wife and a three-bedroom colonial in the suburbs, but I still felt a certain emptiness. My aunt's murder was gnawing at me. I had raised questions about Albert DeSalvo's guilt on television and tried to get the Boston Police Department involved. What more could I do? I was having a difficult time tracking down relatives of any of the ten other strangler victims. I was growing moody and distant at home. Laura was spending all her free time studying for her M.B.A. exams, but she knew I was troubled. "Grab your coat," she ordered one night. "We're going out, and I'm buying you a beer." We discussed my problem over a couple of ice-cold Dos Equis and some nachos at a local tavern. "Listen, honey, you're just at an impasse right now. But things can change quickly," Laura reassured me. "What about DNA? More and more of these old cases are getting solved that way," Laura pointed out. "I know," I said. "They are. Every time I've left a message at the Boston Police Department, I've stressed the possibility of DNA testing. But no one will talk to me. It's weird; it's like everyone at police headquarters ducks for cover when you mention the Boston Strangler."

11 : A Vision in the Night

The morning of July 9, 1999, began for me like most others. I let our new puppy, a golden retriever we called Bailey (after Bailey's Irish Cream not F. Lee Bailey), out for her morning duty. Wearing my bathrobe, sleepy-eyed, and in need of a cup of strong coffee, I walked to the end of our driveway to pick up the morning papers, which I would scour to prepare for my morning conference call with my colleagues at WBZ. That day's *Boston Globe* headline jumped off the page. It read, "POLICE HOPE DNA SCIENCE WILL TELL IF DESALVO WAS '60S-ERA KILLER."

I walked back into the house barely able to breathe. The *Globe* reporter Brian McGrory had written that the Boston Police Department's cold case squad had launched a reinvestigation into the Boston Strangler case. According to the article, the review had been going on for eighteen months. The squad leader, Captain Tim Murray, said he hoped DNA testing would put an end to a decades-old mystery. "The Strangler case is one of the most notorious in the country," Murray told the *Globe*. "If we can solve this, it might spark other cities to use DNA to solve old crimes. There is no statute of limitation on murder."

I had called Murray countless times and never gotten further than his voice mail. "What is going on?" I asked myself.

The phone rang, and I jumped. When I picked it up, I heard my assignment editor, Tom Luft, on the other end. "What the fuck is going on with the strangler?" he asked excitedly. "Honestly, I have no idea. I just found out myself," I told him. Luft put me onto a conference call. My producer colleagues were shocked to hear I had no more information on the story than they did. If the Boston Strangler case was being reopened, it was a major story, and the *Boston Globe* had gotten if before we did. We had ground to make up.

Tom Luft immediately placed a call to the Boston Police Department spokeswoman, Margot Hill. Surprisingly, she would not comment on the story. Apparently, there was a mad scramble going on at police headquarters. Officials there had not wanted this story leaked.

"Commissioner Evans is attending a news conference on racial profiling. We'll get him to talk about the strangler there," Luft shouted across the newsroom. Charlie Austin, a veteran reporter, was covering the racial profiling event. In his three decades at the station, Austin had formed strong bonds with the power players inside the BPD. If he couldn't get Paul Evans to talk, no one else would.

At the news conference, Evans strongly denied there was a new investigation of the Boston Strangler case. He claimed that what looked like a reinvestigation was actually nothing more than a training exercise for members of the police crime lab. He went on to criticize the *Globe* for overzealous reporting and misstating facts. When asked if he had any doubt that Albert DeSalvo was the Boston Strangler, Evans said, "Absolutely not."

The next day, July 10, 1999, I called Margot Hill myself. She told me the department was very sympathetic to my interest in the case but that there was no physical evidence left from the crime scenes to test for DNA. "We're talking about evidence from eleven unsolved murders. Where did it all go?" I asked. "I don't know," Hill replied.

My next call was to the crime lab. I was sure I would get the party line that no reinvestigation of the Boston Strangler murders was in progress or planned for the future. But I got lucky. A technician answered my call and not one of his supervisors. "Hey, man, I'm just looking for a little info on this strangler business," I said casually. "Is it true that you guys have no physical evidence left from any of the crime scenes?" The technician replied, "Who told you that? We have boxes of the stuff." "Yes!" I thought to myself. But I needed clarification. "You mean you have boxes labeled Boston Strangler?" I asked. "That's right, I'm staring at about a dozen of them right now," the technician assured me. Then he said, "Wait, you're not gonna report any of this, right?" He was realizing that he was probably not supposed to be telling me any of this. "No," I said, "your secret is safe with me." I thanked him and hung up. Sitting back at my desk, I digested what I had just heard. Police officials were telling me one thing, but those on the inside knew better.

That evening, I drove to Mom's house in Hyannis to give her an update. It didn't surprise her that law enforcement officials were still playing a shell game when it came to the Boston Strangler. But I sensed there was something else bothering her. "What's the matter, Mom?" I asked. "I . . . I can't say. It sounds ridiculous," she replied. With a little more coaxing, she finally let go. "Mary . . . I saw Mary last night," she said. "Oh, boy," I thought to myself. "Did she come to you in a dream?" I asked, not certain where this conversation was going. "It wasn't a dream. I was in the living room, and she was calling to me from the hallway. I saw her standing right where you're standing, now," Mom replied. "She said, 'Find my murderer . . . find my murderer.'" Mom's voice was breaking. "She was soaking wet, Casey. I don't know why, but she was soaking wet." Mom was crying now. "We have to do it, Case, we have to do whatever we can to find her killer. She won't rest until we do."

I reached out and hugged my mother, searching my mind for the right words. No doubt, the *Boston Globe* story had stirred up intense feelings. But what she had seen was real to her. I told her I loved her and assured her that I would try to find Mary's killer, but I actually had no idea what to do next. As I drove back to Boston the following day, I made a private plea to my dead aunt: All right, Mary, help me out here. What do I do now?"

At work that day I sat at my desk staring blankly at the computer screen. I realized that I had made a promise to my mother that I might not be able to keep. Tom Luft's booming voice shook me from my trance. "Casey—you have a call on the nutline. He's asking for you by name," Luft hollered. The nutline is a general phone number for the newsroom. Usually, nutline callers are either cranks or crazies who phone in to report that a UFO is landing on their front lawn or that Elvis is relaxing in their bathtub.

"Mary, this isn't exactly the kind of help I need right now," I thought as I picked up the phone. I said, "This is Casey Sherman, WBZ-4 news. What can I do for you?" I could barely understand the man on the other end. "You the guy who's investigating the Boston Strangler?" he asked. I confirmed that I was. "My name is Michael De-Salvo. I'm Albert DeSalvo's son," he said. At first, I thought the caller was lying, but he knew many details of the case and said he had gotten my name from his Uncle Richard. I told Michael to call me back in a few minutes, after I'd confirmed his story with his uncle. Then I phoned Richard, who told me he had given my name to his nephew. "You should watch him, though; he's got problems," warned Richard.

I knew Albert DeSalvo had two children, but no one had ever interviewed either of them. Michael called back. He said, "I wanna clear my Dad's name, and I want you to help." I offered to meet him that night at a bar in Quincy, just a couple of miles south of Boston. After he agreed to the meeting, I almost hung up the phone, but then I stopped myself. "Oh, by the way, I don't know what you look like. How will I find you at the bar?" I asked. "That's easy," Michael replied. "I look just like my dad."

12 : Here Comes the Son

I called my wife and told her I'd be a little late coming home because of my meeting with Michael DeSalvo. "Be careful; this guy could be a real nut, honey," Laura advised. Her concern quickly turned into panic. "Make sure you park under a streetlight with some other cars around. Are you sure you want to do this?" she asked. "This guy's legit. Don't worry about me. I'll be fine," I reassured her.

Inside, however, I did have concerns about my safety. After work, I drove ten minutes south to Quincy and pulled into the large parking lot outside The Fours, a sports pub known for its steak tips and wide selection of brews. DeSalvo had told me he had a white van and I pulled up next to it.

He gave me a quick nod through the window, and we both stepped slowly out of our vehicles. "Don't talk to me. They could be watching us," he said softly. I glanced casually over my shoulder but saw no one there. Inside, Michael picked a quiet spot at the end of the bar. The Red

Sox had the night off, and the sports bar was virtually empty. "Well, Mike," I said, "I've had a hell of a day and could sure use a beer right now. What do you want? I'm buying." Michael began fidgeting with his cigarette lighter. He said, "Just water, thank you." I ordered a Bud Light for myself and a spring water for him. After that we sat there in awkward silence, Michael's eyes moving around the bar. Finally, he said, "It's my girlfriend; I think she's having me followed. She didn't want me to meet you here tonight." I nodded my head. Should I excuse myself, go the men's room, and get the hell out of here? No, I owe it to my mother to hear him out.

This man had his demons, that was obvious. I studied his face under the bright lights of the bar. Michael De-Salvo had been cursed with his father's infamous profile. Though he had long hair and a mustache, he clearly was Albert DeSalvo's son, with his father's brown eyes and his long, hooked nose. We had been sitting now for fifteen minutes, and I decided that I'd had enough of the silence. "All right, Michael, I'm here," I said. "Now tell me exactly what you want me to do for you."

For the next two hours, the thirty-seven-year-old man told me his story. "I never knew who my dad was," he began. "I grew up on a U.S. Army base in Germany thinking my name was Mike Nichols. My mom remarried and never once talked about my real father. It wasn't until I was eighteen years old and trying to get into the army that I found out the truth. They [army officials] wouldn't accept my identification papers, so my mom had to produce my real birth certificate. A staff sergeant asked me if I knew who my real dad was. I said I did not. The sergeant told me that my father was the Boston Strangler." Michael lit a cigarette, and I noticed his hand begin to shake. Here was another living victim of the Boston Strangler case. "Damn Albert DeSalvo," I thought to myself. "Just look at what you and your lies did to your own son."

"What did you do after the army, Michael?" I asked.

"Well, I had some rough times. I thought my dad was this serial killer, and I thought he could have passed it along to me. I thought I might inherit the desire to kill someone." Michael told me he had spent most of his adult life drifting from state to state, abusing drugs and alcohol. "When I finally came here to Massachusetts, I found out where my old man was buried and went up to visit him with a bottle of vodka in my hand," he continued, a tear beginning to form at the corner of his eye. "I was drunk and got down on my knees and started clawing at the dirt around his grave. I wanted to dig my dad up and strangle him myself. I really hated the bastard."

Michael credited the television program *Unsolved Mysteries* with changing his point of view. He said, "I watched it and, for the first time, I heard people say he didn't do it. I started to read up on it, and I now believe that he was sick and that F. Lee Bailey manipulated him to confess to these awful crimes."

"I think you have a strong story to tell, and I'd be glad to help you tell it . . . if you're up to it," I promised. I gave Michael my card and a firm handshake and told him to call me when he was ready.

It was several weeks before Michael felt comfortable enough to do the interview. He had discovered sobriety, and he was very proud of the fact that he had not had a drink in several months. Still, I was hesitant about putting him in front of the camera. I was not sure he was up to it emotionally. But he felt it was his duty to dispel the myths about his father. Michael voiced his own reservations, however. "I'm coming out in the public, but what if no one listens to what I have to say? The people will just see my face and say, 'There's the son of the strangler.' What do I do then? You gotta promise me that won't happen," he said, grabbing my leather jacket. "Michael, you've done nothing wrong here," I replied. "People will sympathize with your cause. You've got to trust me on this."

"Can I trust you? Can I really trust you?" he asked.

"I know the pain you're going through. I know it better than any other journalist you'll ever meet. You lost your father, and I lost my aunt. My mother lost her sister. Yes, Michael, you can trust me," I assured him.

I had given it my best shot. If he said no to the interview now, I was ready to walk away. I was not going to encourage him to do something he did not want to do.

My colleague Ted Wayman, a WBZ reporter, conducted the interview in October 1999, and I produced it. Michael was biting his fingernails and fidgeting before the cameras rolled. However, when the lights went on and the photographer signaled that the videotape was rolling, Michael pleaded his case to the camera exceptionally well. "I will go to any length to clear my dad's name," Michael said emphatically. Michael said he would be willing to give his own blood for DNA testing in hopes of exonerating his father. "My dad did some bad things, but he was no serial killer." Wayman and I both agreed that the interview was a smashing success. Michael DeSalvo pointed the finger of guilt at his father's former attorney, F. Lee Bailey.

Our next step was to take Michael back to his father's

grave site, where he had gone in a drunken rage many years before. We drove to the Puritan Lawn Cemetery in Peabody. It was a beautiful autumn day, with multicolored leaves falling from the trees. A big problem for us was that Albert DeSalvo's grave did not have a headstone but it was instead marked by a small plaque that was tucked away along a row of other markers. We spent the better part of an afternoon kicking up the leaves, searching for Albert DeSalvo's grave. When at last we found the marker, Michael stood silently for several moments before he spoke. "I want to walk around with my head held high. I want to help the families of the victims," he said, choking back tears.

WBZ ran Michael DeSalvo's interview on our 11:00 P.M. newscast on November 7, 1999. The *Globe* and its tabloid competitor, the *Herald,* ran stories about Michael's interview in their morning editions on November 8. The other local TV stations clamored for interviews with Michael. When I called Michael to congratulate him, no one answered. "He probably needs some time to himself," I figured, but knowing how fragile Michael was at the time, I could not help worrying. My colleague the reporter Charlie Austin caught up with Massachusetts Attorney General Tom Reilly on November 9 and asked him about the possibility of reopening the Boston Strangler case. Reilly pointed out that his office had never charged DeSalvo with any of the strangler murders. What he seemed to forget was that his predecessor Edward Brooke had sold the public on DeSalvo's guilt. Reilly added that he would be willing to meet with the strangler victims' families to discuss their concerns.

A few hours after this interview, the attorney general telephoned me in the newsroom and asked me to state my case. Tom Reilly, I knew, was politically astute, but he had not been getting the attention he yearned for. I told him my Aunt Mary was said to have been the final victim in the Boston Strangler case. I also explained why I had serious doubts regarding the guilt of Albert DeSalvo. The soft-spoken Reilly said he was not familiar with the history of the case, but he offered to look at the Boston Strangler files and see if there was sufficient cause for a reinvestigation. "I'll put my top guy on it, and he'll get back to you," Reilly told me.

Several days after the story on Michael DeSalvo ran, I still hadn't heard from Michael, though I had left a number of messages on his answering machine. I had given him a private screening of our story before it aired, and he said he liked it, so he couldn't be angry at me, I thought. Finally, I received a call from a nurse at a local psychiatric hospital. Michael DeSalvo was back in rehab. "He claims he's the son of Albert DeSalvo," the nurse informed me. "He's not delusional," I told her. "He's exactly who he says he is. Can I speak with him?"

Michael got on the phone. "Hey, buddy," he mumbled.

"Michael, what's going on . . . what happened?" I asked.

"It happened," he replied. "I was walking down my street the day after the show aired and this little kid pointed at me and said, 'There's the Boston Strangler!'" Michael was crying now. "I just walked past him and straight to the package store, and now here I am. I'm so sorry."

"No, Michael, I'm sorry," I replied. "I made you a promise, and I let you down." I told Michael not to worry about the case and that his only concern was getting well. After I hung up, I slammed my knuckles down hard on the desk. I had known he was vulnerable. I should have done more to protect him. I vowed never to place Michael DeSalvo in that position again.

Now that WBZ-TV had revived it, reporters all over the city were competing for a fresh angle on the Boston Strangler story. With Michael in hiding now, they were forced to call upon people associated with the case to get their point of view. The *Herald* quoted Dr. Ames Robey as saying he was in favor of exhuming Albert DeSalvo's body for DNA testing. The paper also interviewed Jim Mellon. I had read about Mellon several times in connection with my aunt's case, but I had never been able to track him down. I thought Mellon had died, but according to the *Herald* the seventy-five-year-old retired police officer was living in Marshfield, which, coincidentally, was F. Lee Bailey's hometown. While I was driving along Route 3 caught in heavy traffic heading into the city, I dialed 411 on my cell phone on the off chance that Mellon's number was listed. It was. When I reached him at his house, I could tell by the sound of his weary voice that he'd already been flooded with interview requests.

I said, "Mr. Mellon, I would love to send a reporter to your home to do a follow-up on our story, but more important, I'd like to meet you myself."

"Why all the interest in this case, young man?" he asked.

"Sir, my aunt was Mary Sullivan. My mother has lived for nearly forty years with the belief that her sister's killer was never caught. I happen to believe she's right."

Mellon paused a moment. "Oh, yes, Mary Sullivan . . . that poor girl. I was one of the first officers to arrive at her apartment that night. Awful—it was just awful."

I asked him if he had any idea who may have killed Mary. "Well, I don't think these murders were all done by the same guy," Mellon answered. "But in her case, I'm positive it was a boyfriend of one of her roommates."

I offered up the name Joseph Preston Moss. "That's your guy," Mellon said. "You find him, you'll find her killer."

I kept Jim Mellon on the phone that morning for a full hour. He told me he had remained on the police force for twenty years after my aunt's murder, with much of his career spent walking the beat in some of Boston's toughest neighborhoods. "I was passed over when it came to promotions, and it was all because I wouldn't play ball on the strangler case," Mellon told me. Since his retirement from the Boston Police Department in 1985, he and his wife had lived comfortably on his pension in their home just a few yards from the ocean.

"My kids get a kick out of the fact their old man was involved in something like that," he said, referring to the Boston Strangler case. But then he brought the conversation back to the victims, the way he always did. "Those poor girls," he said. "What happened to them was horrible. And what happened afterwards was just as bad." Mellon's voice trailed off. At first, I thought I was having problems with my cell phone. But then I realized the investigator had traveled back nearly forty years in his mind. Mellon was picturing himself inside my aunt's apartment. He saw the broomstick on gruesome display. He saw the Happy New Year card next to Mary's foot.

"As I said, young man, you find Preston Moss, and you'll find the real killer!" Mellon finally said.

"Can I call on you for help?" I asked.

"Sure, son, I'll be right here."

13 : The Ghost from Christmas Past

It was time to find Preston Moss. I knew he had grown up in the Boston suburb of Arlington and attended Boston University for one year. Mellon told me he had last had contact with Moss in December 1964. After authorities focused on Albert DeSalvo, Preston Moss dropped out of college and out of sight.

My first course of action was to visit my friends on the I-Team, the investigative arm of WBZ-4 news. Tucked away in their tiny, cluttered office, team members reporter Joe Bergantino and producer Paul Toomey are Boston's version of Bob Woodward and Carl Bernstein. The I-Team has alerted the public to priest abuse in the Catholic Church and uncovered cost overruns in the Big Dig project, the largest highway construction project in history. The team has all sorts of investigative tools at their fingertips. Using one of these, a computer program called Auto-Tracker, you can type in a person's name, and if that person has ever applied for a driver's license, his full name, the town he lives in, and his phone number pop up on the screen. There could be only one Joseph Preston Moss out there, and an Auto-Tracker search for him was certainly worth a shot. Paul Toomey typed in Moss's name, and the program produced a result in seconds. There on the computer screen was the name Joseph Preston Moss. He was still living in New England.

Jotting down Moss's phone number and current address, I walked back to my desk, picked up the phone, and started dialing the number. I was about to speak with the man who may have murdered my aunt. What would I say? I let the telephone ring a couple of times and then abruptly hung up. Clearly, I was not prepared for this conversation. I told myself I'd call him when I got home.

In my kitchen that evening, I stared at the tiny piece of paper with the phone number on it, rolling it back and forth between my fingers. I still wasn't ready to place the call. I stayed up late into the night, examining every piece of information I had on my aunt's murder. Was Moss really the killer? I had thought for a long time that Nathan Ward, Mary's former boyfriend, was the strongest suspect. Ward's volatile relationship with Mary and their sudden breakup offered a motive. There were also discrepancies in his alibi.

Jim Mellon thought Ward was a flake, but he didn't believe he was responsible for Mary's murder. Mellon thought Moss was a much more likely suspect. He believed Moss was sexually repressed and angry at Delmore for refusing to have sex with him. Was it because Delmore was seeing someone else, or was it because the apartment was too crowded for any chance of intimacy? Mellon thought Moss blamed Mary for this. What did I know about this Preston Moss character? The fact that he had failed two lie detector tests disturbed me. And why had Moss been so interested in the police investigation of Mary's death?

The next morning, I went about my routine as if nothing was bothering me. While I sipped my coffee and my wife, Laura, drank her Diet Coke, she asked me if I was doing anything interesting that day. I told her no. At this point, there was no need to worry her. I waited for her to leave for work before I picked up the telephone and made the call. "Here goes nothing." I said to myself. The phone rang three times, and a woman answered. I introduced myself as a journalist from Boston and told her who I was looking for.

"What's this about?" the woman asked.

"I'd just like to ask him some questions for a story I'm working on," I replied. She barked Moss's name, and a few seconds later, he picked up the telephone. Introducing myself as a Boston journalist but not mentioning my family connection to Mary, I said, "I'd like to ask you some questions about the Boston Strangler case, specifically about the murder of Mary Sullivan." Moss gasped. Then for several seconds there was an awkward silence. It was as if the ghost from Christmas past had just appeared at his bedside.

Moss finally broke the silence. "Didn't they get the guy?" he asked nervously.

"No, not yet," I replied. "But the good thing about this case is that there's no statute of limitations on murder. In fact, weren't you once considered the prime suspect?" When Moss did not answer, I asked again. "Isn't it true, Preston, that you failed two lie detector tests?"

"Yes, but it was way back in the sixties. Those things aren't scientific."

"You're absolutely right," I replied, doing my best Colombo imitation. "But I got to tell you. There are some people who are convinced you're the guy. I know if I was being accused of a heinous crime, I'd do whatever it took to clear my name. Preston, would you be willing to take a DNA test to settle this matter?"

"No!" Moss shot back, his voice getting louder. "I'm not gonna take any test unless there's a court order."

"One may be coming for you some day, Preston, so I'd watch out if I were you," I advised. Moss slammed the phone down.

I ran through the conversation in my mind. He's definitely concerned about something, I decided. I would let my words sink in a bit before trying to contact him again. I had worried him, and, I must admit, it felt good.

When I got to work that day, there was a message for me to call Assistant Attorney General Gerry Leone. It was now late November 1999. I told Leone everything about the case that I thought was important, including my conversation with Moss. Leone promised to take a fresh look at the Boston Strangler files and then to meet with my family. I told him my mother had waited nearly forty years to get answers to the questions about her sister's murder, and a few more months wouldn't hurt us.

Nonetheless, I knew that to get the full attention of the attorney general's office, I needed help from the family of Albert DeSalvo. I also knew Michael was still struggling with personal problems and would be in no shape to meet with the state's top law enforcement officials. It was time, then, to call Richard DeSalvo once more. My pitch to Richard took a more urgent tone this time around. I told him the state of Massachusetts was taking the Boston Strangler case seriously again, but that time was running out. "It's now or never, Richard," I warned. "We need to get this done while many of the key players are still alive."

This time, Richard DeSalvo was up to the challenge.

"What the hell, Casey, let's do it," he said.

14 : An Alliance Is Born

Richard DeSalvo and I formed a most unusual alliance: the family of an accused serial killer joining forces with the family of his last alleged victim in a search for the truth. Although we were now a team, we had different goals, however. I wanted to find my aunt's killer; to do so I would have to exonerate Albert DeSalvo. Richard wanted to clear his family name, not so much for his brother's sake but for his young grandchildren. He simply wanted the stigma removed from his family's name.

Back at the station, I got word that Edward Brooke was back in Boston and wanted to talk about the Boston Strangler case. Brooke was writing his autobiography and was trying to drum up attention. My colleagues and I thought it best that I not conduct the interview because my personal stake in the story could pose a conflict of interest. Again, I relied on my friend the veteran reporter Charlie Austin to be my voice.

Austin caught up with the retired politician at his

Boston office and asked him about the new developments in the case. "Do you think the case should be reopened?" Austin inquired.

"If it would not bring more pain and suffering to victims' families, I certainly would have no objection to it," Brooke answered.

Austin asked Brooke if he had gotten the right man.

The answer was startling. "If you ask me if I'm convinced that Albert DeSalvo was the Boston Strangler," Brooke said, "I can't tell them [the victims' families]. I can't give them a definitive answer."

This was coming from one of the staunchest proponents of DeSalvo's guilt, the man who, along with F. Lee Bailey, had sold the public the idea that DeSalvo was the strangler. Now, forty years later, Brooke was saying he was not sure? "If you had doubts, you should've voiced them back then instead of leaving me with this big mess now!" I yelled at the television monitor when I first viewed the videotape of the interview.

Still, I realized that my goal was not to point a finger at former public officials. What I wanted to do was work with the current administration to find my aunt's killer. Over the next months, Assistant Attorney General Leone and I continued what I thought were positive conversations about the case. Not your stereotypical glad-handing, baby-kissing politician, Leone, a former marine, never seemed comfortable around other people. In me this quality engendered trust. I believed Leone and I were both committed to finding the answers to the decades-old murder mystery.

The mounting pressures of the investigation were nothing compared to the pressures at home. Laura was pregnant with our first child. But our immediate joy turned to concern when an ultrasound test revealed that my wife had an ovarian tumor. Telling us that surgery was the only option, the gynecologist said he was confident our baby could survive the procedure, but he could offer no guarantee.

In February 2000, Laura, two months pregnant, went in for surgery, and all my attention shifted from the Boston Strangler case to the health of my wife and our unborn child. While Laura was in the operating room, I prayed as I'd never prayed before, staring up to the heavens and imploring God to please keep Laura and the baby safe. Two hours after the procedure began, the surgeon met me in the waiting room and told me Laura's tumor had been successfully removed and that she was doing fine. However, it was still too early to tell if our baby had survived. In the recovery room I held Laura's hand while she slept. Tears filling my eyes, I leaned over my wife's belly. "You have a brave mommy who loves you very much," I whispered to my unborn child.

The next morning, Laura and I waited silently in her hospital room for the doctor. Did we still have our baby? When he arrived, he checked Laura's vital signs and then placed the stethoscope on her stomach. The baby's tiny heart was beating strongly. Laura and I looked at each other, smiling. Then I looked up at the ceiling and said, "Thank you."

During the next few weeks, I cared for my wife at home with the help of my mom and mother-in-law. At the same time, I was finalizing plans for a meeting in the attorney general's office in which I also wanted the Boston Police Department to participate. (Before the case had been taken over by the state, the police homicide squad had been in charge of investigating Mary's murder.) Two days before the meeting, I finally received a call back from the police official in charge of the homicide division and also head of the cold case squad. When I asked him if he could attend the meeting, he said, "No, we won't be there. And if I were you, I'd stay away from this case."

"Why is that?" I asked, dumbfounded.

"Casey, this case is a lot bigger than just a bunch of strangled women."

"Lieutenant, I know it's bigger. But what are you trying to tell me?" I was angry now. There was a pause on the other end of the phone. The official now seemed to realize that he had let a few indiscreet words slip out. He said, "We don't want to set a precedent here. It's not the purpose of the cold case squad to go back and reinvestigate unsolved murders."

My pale Irish cheeks were flushed red now. "Then what is the purpose of the cold case squad, and how much of my tax dollars are going into it if you're sitting around playing cards all day?"

The police official ignored my outburst. He said, "We just don't think it's in the best interest of the families involved, that's all."

I reminded him that he was talking with a member of one of the families and that we demanded justice, but that didn't change his mind about participating in the meeting. I was left wondering what the Boston Police Department was so afraid of.

Gerry Leone had set the meeting for March 13, 2000. I had told him that my mother and I would be there, along with members of Albert DeSalvo's family. Hearing from the families was important, but I believed that we also needed input from one of the people who had worked on the case. I dialed Jim Mellon's number.

"Mr. Mellon, can I call you to duty one more time?" I asked after telling him about the meeting.

"You've certainly stirred up quite a storm," Mellon said. "You go public, and they'll come after you." Mellon did not need to explain who "they" were.

"Why are they so worried about this case, Jim?"

Mellon paused before answering. "Son, this isn't just about the Boston Strangler. Oh, sure, it's the biggest case of them all. But what about the would-be Albert De-Salvos out there? The suspects who were pressured to confess to a crime they didn't commit. The state has a finger in the dike right now, but once they pull that finger out, the flooding begins."

It was a colorful way of saying that if we showed that authorities had gotten the wrong guy in the biggest murder case in New England history, it could call into question thousands of other cases the state claimed had been solved.

"Can I count on you to be there?" I asked Mellon.

"Oh sure," he laughed, "us against the state. I like those odds. Plus it will get me out of the house for the afternoon."

Now that I had gotten Jim Mellon's promise to attend the meeting, I needed to make sure that the public was aware of the event. I pitched the idea to my news director, and he decided to allow a reporter, Ted Wayman, to cover the story. No matter what the outcome of the meeting was, at least our viewers would know that an attempt to reopen this case had been made by the families.

On the day of the Strangler Summit, I met Jim Mellon at a South Shore parking lot and drove him into the city. He wore his traditional Irish scally cap and walking sneakers for climbing the steep hills around Boston's

Government Center. My mother sat in the back of my Chevy Blazer, fidgeting with her bracelet.

The Massachusetts attorney general's office is located at One Ashburton Place, behind the statehouse. That day, the streets were lined with parked cars and the lots filled to capacity, so I was forced to park downhill about a quarter mile away, and Mellon's walking shoes gave him little help as he slowly made his way up the steep sidewalks of Beacon Hill. Finally, I offered to retrieve the car and drop him off in front of the building, but he declined, determined to make it on his own. Breathing hard at the start, he caught a second wind, and we made it to the attorney general's office with time to spare. During our walk, the retired policeman enlivened the conversation with stories about patrolling the city at the time of the Boston Strangler. It felt good to have him back on the case.

Before the meeting started, I told my television crew that no cameras would be allowed inside the attorney general's office, but we would be available for comment after the meeting. Then Gerry Leone's secretary showed us into a conference room; the DeSalvos arrived shortly after. It was the first time my mother had ever come face to face with a relative of the alleged Boston Strangler. Though obviously uncomfortable, she nonetheless managed a gracious hello. Pulling her aside, I told her everything was going to be okay and reminded her that the DeSalvos were innocent victims, too.

After several more minutes, Gerry Leone finally arrived, alone.

"Isn't the Attorney General going to be here?" I asked.

"Tom's really busy and usually doesn't attend these kind of meetings," Leone replied. I introduced the family

members to Leone and announced that I had also brought
along a special guest, the man who had investigated my
aunt's murder in 1964. After a quick nod to Jim Mellon,
Leone asked me to state our case briefly. Clearly, he was
trying to indicate that he was pressed for time. I reminded
Leone that Albert DeSalvo never had been charged with
my aunt's murder or any of the other killings attributed to
the Boston Strangler. I also discussed the lack of physical
evidence against DeSalvo. Jim Mellon added that he and
his colleagues on the Boston Strangler Task Force knew
that DeSalvo was not "the guy."

"Do you have any new evidence?" Leone asked, apparently unmoved by our presentation.

"There is no new evidence," I replied. "It's all there in
the old evidence. You read the case files, Gerry. There
was a prime suspect in Mary's murder, and his name is
not Albert DeSalvo. I know where this suspect is. What's
it going to take to capture the real killer?"

"Murder investigations are not really something we do
here in the attorney general's office," Leone said, de-
flecting the question.

"Your office took jurisdiction over this case after my
aunt was killed," I reminded him. "It's your responsibil-
ity to see it through!"

"Well, right now the Boston Police Department says it
has no more physical evidence from the murder of Mary
Sullivan. Boston says the case is no longer a priority. We
defer to them. There's really nothing we can do for you
here," Leone replied.

"I was told by a Boston police official just yesterday
to stay away from this case. I was told that it was a lot
bigger than a bunch of strangled women. Is there something that no one wants us to find out here?" I fired back.

"There's no conspiracy going on here," Leone answered. "And besides, does anyone really believe De-Salvo was the strangler anymore?"

My mother's eyes lit up at Leone's comment. "What do you mean, does anybody believe it? Everyone still thinks he did it, and my government allowed it to happen," Mom said, pointing to Leone.

Richard DeSalvo and his son Tim jumped in, telling Leone about the harassment they had endured for decades. Richard also said he would like to know who had killed his brother. "I think someone did it to shut him up, and the prison guards were involved," he said.

Leone was not swayed. He claimed his hands were tied because the Boston Police Department had no interest in revisiting this case. Then we were shown out of the conference room.

"They don't want to touch it," Mellon said to me in the hallway. But if Leone thought we would just go away, he was dead wrong. Waiting for us down the hall were Ted Wayman and Dick Ade, a WBZ photographer.

"What happened in there, Diane?" Wayman asked my mother, the camera rolling.

"He said there was no evidence left to find my sister's killer. I've only got one question, where did all the evidence go?" she asked in disbelief.

She knew that the crime lab had confirmed to me that it had a dozen boxes of physical materials taken from the crime scenes. Either Leone knew this, or someone wasn't telling him the truth.

I told Wayman we would revisit the case ourselves. I also floated the idea of exhuming my aunt's body and the body of Albert DeSalvo to see if there was any DNA that would exonerate or incriminate DeSalvo. At this time, I did not know much about forensic science or how to begin such a project. I was bluffing to see how the authorities would respond.

The attorney general's office offered only a brief written statement on the meeting. "At this time we do not anticipate any further role for this office in the matter," it said. Meanwhile, the Boston police spokeswoman, Margot Hill, told the *Herald* she sympathized with the families. "We feel for them," she said, "and we share in their frustration, but we don't have a probative sample of DNA to go forward."

On the drive back to the South Shore, Mellon did his best to keep Mom's spirits up. But I felt defeated. The state with all its resources claimed it could not help us. When I dropped Mellon off at his car, we spoke for a few minutes.

"Sorry I wasted your time, Jim," I said.

"Don't give up, son," he replied. "If I've learned one thing in my life, it's that you can't give up on something you believe in. You're doing the right thing here. You've got to force their hand, Casey. You've got to keep giving them hell, son," Mellon said before he climbed into his car and drove away.

15 : On Our Own

That evening, I grabbed an ice-cold bottle of Dos Equis and collapsed on the living room couch, trying to unwind from my long day and deal with my doubts about the future of the case. Laura, regaining strength after her surgery, joined me in the living room. I took the remote control and flipped through the television channels, finally settling on a Discovery Channel documentary about the forensic reinvestigation of the Jesse James case. The notorious outlaw had reportedly been gunned down in 1882 by a member of his own gang, but in later years several men came forward claiming to be James. Had Jesse James faked his own death? That's what his descendants wanted to know. In 1995, a forensic team led by a George Washington University law professor named James Starrs exhumed the body buried under Jesse James's tombstone in Kearney, Missouri. By comparing hair samples from the gunslinger's great-granddaughter to those taken from the remains, Starrs and his team determined with 99.7 percent certainty that the body was that of Jesse James.

Professor Starrs was featured heavily in the television program. "Why don't you call this guy?" Laura asked. "I bet he could help you. You have a high profile case, too. I'm sure he'd be interested." How could it hurt? I decided. The next morning, I called Professor Starrs.

James Starrs, the son of an English professor and an art teacher, grew up near New York City and early on developed a love for Sir Arthur Conan Doyle's master sleuth, Sherlock Holmes. After earning a law degree from St. John's University, Starrs began his teaching career at George Washington University in 1964, the year of my aunt's murder. In the late 1960s, Starrs was asked to lead a new forensic science master's program at the university. As a result, he became a real-life equivalent to his literary hero, Sherlock Holmes.

Once I got Starrs on the phone, I asked if he knew anything about the Boston Strangler case.

"You mean Al Salvi?" Starrs replied. I took Starrs's mistake as a good sign. It indicated to me that he likely did not have a preconception about Albert DeSalvo's guilt or innocence. "What exactly are you looking for, Mr. Sherman?" Starrs asked.

I told him about my connection with the case and said, "I don't believe DeSalvo murdered my aunt, but I'm getting nowhere with the authorities here. We're not looking for fame, we're not looking for money. We just want justice. I need to know if it would be possible to find evidence of her killer on my aunt's body?"

Starrs went on to tell me there were several factors that could help or hurt a forensic examination of my aunt's remains. "If she were shot, I'd say you were out of luck. But the fact that she was strangled indicates that her killer could have left hair, blood, or saliva on her body," he pointed out. It upset me to hear my aunt's murder talked about so coldly, but science had no room for emotions, and I would have to get used to it.

Starrs told me that he would be interested in getting involved in the case, but before signing on to such a project, he needed to know everything possible about Mary's burial. I promised I would get the information he required. Still, the thought of exhuming my aunt's body was troubling. Was there any other option?

"Professor, I know the state of Massachusetts still has evidence left from my aunt's murder. If we sued for it, would we have much of a case?"

"I'd much rather work with evidence that already exists. An exhumation is always the last resort," Starrs replied. "But if this case is indeed closed, I don't see why you or your mother would not be entitled to the materials."

"Do you know of any good lawyers in the Boston area?" I asked. I wanted an attorney Starrs would be comfortable working with. He advised me to speak with a friend of his, an attorney named Elaine Whitfield Sharp. Starrs probably did not know this, but Sharp was considered Attorney General Tom Reilly's arch-nemesis. They had faced each other when Reilly was a district attorney prosecuting the Louise Woodward case, in which Woodward, a British au pair, had been accused of murdering an infant in her care. A British native herself, Sharp felt it her duty to defend the young woman, and she and her lawyer husband, Dan Sharp, masterminded the medical defense in the case, producing medical experts to dispute the existence of the so-called shaken-baby syndrome. However, she was probably best known to the public as the attorney who had hugged and consoled Woodward while the young woman sobbed uncontrollably when the guilty verdict came down.

Starrs was highly complimentary of Sharp's work, but I wasn't so sure she was the right person for the job. Following Louise Woodward's conviction, Sharp had quit the defense team and was later arrested for drunken driving. She then accused the arresting officer of sexual harassment. (That accusation would come back to haunt the attorney. In 2003, Sharp was found liable of defaming the officer and ordered to pay $208,000 in damages. The verdict is currently under appeal.) I questioned whether she was stable enough to take on the case. Out of respect for Starrs, however, I agreed to meet with the Sharps at their law office in the historic seaside town of Marblehead.

As I drove to the meeting, on a Sunday afternoon in late March 2000, I drove through Chelsea, Albert DeSalvo's birthplace. I drove through Lynn, where Helen Blake had met a horrible death. I drove through Salem, where Evelyn Corbin had been strangled. Finally, I arrived in the town of Marblehead. Elaine Whitfield Sharp met me with a smile at the office door and ushered me into their conference room. Dan Sharp was already sitting there with a notepad and pen in his hand. I could tell immediately that the couple was a contrast in styles. The boisterous Elaine reminded me of a matron at a British boarding school—friendly, but you would not want to cross her. Dan was more of an introvert, a person who chose his words carefully. One thing was clear in any case. Elaine Whitfield Sharp was neither shaky nor uncertain of herself. What I saw was an extremely intelligent person who was strong enough to take on the most powerful people in Massachusetts.

I told the couple I believed that my aunt's killer was

still at large and that Massachusetts authorities were withholding evidence and information about her murder. After I finished, they nodded to me and then began talking to each other as if I weren't there. They sparred for several minutes, citing various cases to deflate each other's analysis. I found it unusual, but it appeared to be effective. In time, they arrived at a common position: that since there was no longer an active investigation into Mary's murder, her family had a right to both physical and documentary evidence. "The evidence should be considered Mary's personal property and therefore be handed over to her family," Elaine concluded. The Sharps agreed to take my family on as clients and urged me to get the DeSalvo family involved as well.

"There's one question that still bugs me," Dan said before I left. "After all these years, why now?"

I said, "Dan, there's no statute of limitations on murder. Would you not want a Nazi war criminal brought to justice regardless of his age? People should be held accountable for their crimes no matter how much time has gone by."

"You just said the right answer, Casey," Dan said. "Guess what? You'll be the family spokesman."

By the time I left their office, I was confident that Elaine and Dan Sharp were the right attorneys for me. Both were well versed in police corruption cases, and they conducted their work outside the old-boy network of Boston legal circles. I phoned Richard DeSalvo's son, Tim, and urged him to meet with Elaine Whitfield Sharp. I was told by both the attorneys and the DeSalvos that the meeting went extremely well. Thereafter, the Sharps and I spent hours together and on the phone planning our legal strategy. We began by sending requests to the five investigative parties in my aunt's murder: the attorney general's office, the Boston Police Department, the Suffolk County district attorney's office, the Massachusetts State Police, and the state medical examiner's office. Each had been involved in the original investigation and could still possess vital information and physical evidence that could help us prove our case. Relying on the Fair Information Practices Act and Freedom of Information Act, the Sharps demanded that all evidence in the Boston Strangler case be turned over to the families of Mary Sullivan and Albert DeSalvo.

None of us believed that the five parties involved in the original investigation would hand over the evidence without a drawn-out fight. In the meantime, I needed something to demonstrate publicly that our cause was just. It had to be big, and it had to be irrefutable. The biggest piece of evidence in the case I could think of was Albert DeSalvo's confession, the only thing that connected him to the crimes. John Bottomly had taped his lengthy interviews with DeSalvo and then reportedly hidden the original tapes in a bank vault. There were also rumors that copies of those tapes existed.

The answer lay not far away from Mary's grave. My mother reminded me that she had once heard about a Cape Cod police officer involved in my aunt's murder case. The Barnstable County sheriff, Nick Eldredge, had been asked to question witnesses in the Hyannis area following Mary's murder. He and his deputy, Tom O'Malley, jumped at the chance to work on such a high-profile case. But that raised a question. There was not much in the way of crime on Cape Cod back in the 1960s. Nick Eldredge was the man you wanted to see when a lobster trap went missing, but could he investigate a murder?

Tom O'Malley's wife said her husband and Eldredge had once been invited to Boston to discuss the DeSalvo confession with their big city colleagues. The meeting broke up early because of some emergency, and the cops from Cape Cod found themselves alone in the conference room. One of the Boston officers had forgotten to take back some of the tapes of DeSalvo's confession, and when Nick Eldredge realized no one was coming back for the tapes, he stuffed them in his jacket and headed home to the Cape. Surprisingly, no one ever came looking for the tapes, and Eldredge held on to them for the next thirty years. Nearing death in the mid-1990s, Tom O'Malley had told my mother the story. "Everybody thinks I have the tapes, but I don't. Nick Eldredge has the tapes," O'-Malley claimed.

Eldredge was still living on Cape Cod. After retiring from the sheriff's department, he had run a successful private detective agency for several years. I telephoned him, explained who I was, and asked if he still had this piece of strangler history. Though very guarded on the phone, he finally admitted that he still had the tapes. When I asked how he had gotten them, he claimed copies were handed out to many police officials who worked the case.

Before I stood a chance of hearing the confession for myself, I needed to gain Eldredge's confidence. On the phone I praised his long and distinguished career and asked him to meet with me. Eldredge agreed to the get-together, but he would make no guarantee about the tapes. He would not even meet me at his home; instead, he chose a parking lot in Hyannis.

Despite his advanced age, Nick Eldredge was still an imposing figure. He was tall with large, powerful hands; I winced as he took my hand and squeezed it. The day of our meeting in the parking lot, Eldredge was wearing a gray windbreaker with a pin prominently displayed on the lapel.

"What is the pin for?" I asked.

"I'm still a deputy sheriff, and I could get called back to duty at any time, so let's make this quick," he replied proudly.

"So, Nick," I said, "where do you want to talk? We could grab a cup of coffee somewhere."

"Oh, no," he said, looking around the parking lot. "I've got just the place. Follow me."

Hopping in my Blazer, I pulled behind Eldredge's sedan. I sat behind him for a full five minutes until the road was clear enough for him to venture out. We drove around Hyannis for almost half an hour, Eldredge keeping a steady pace of about twenty miles an hour. Where the hell was he taking me? I couldn't tell if he was trying to throw someone off his trail, of if he simply had forgotten where he was going. Finally, though, we pulled into the "Bat Cave," the Senior Citizens Center of Hyannis. Eldredge took another five minutes to park, throwing his car into reverse, then forward, until it was just right— right in the middle of two spaces, that is. As he got out of the car, I noticed that he had a thick folder tucked under his arm. Inside, he asked the woman at the front desk if we could have a private room. She nodded, but warned us that the bridge club had reserved the room in forty minutes, so we'd have to hurry. We started with some small talk. Eldredge told me that he wanted to sell the DeSalvo tapes and cash in on his work on the case. He also asked me if I wanted to write a book with him. I shrugged and said anything was possible. My eyes were focused on the folder. "Nick, can I take a look at that?" I asked.

"Not yet," he replied, putting one large hand on top of the manila file.

"Look, Nick, I'm not here to pass judgment on your work in this case. I simply want to find out if DeSalvo is guilty or innocent. I just want to make sure justice was done for Mary."

Eldredge's grip on the folder loosened; then he took out a couple of documents for me to see. One was particularly interesting. Dated January 22, 1964, it was a five-page list of evidence taken from my aunt's apartment by the Boston Police homicide unit. The list contained 245 items. Had the police department lost 245 pieces of evidence? The list included a charm bracelet my mother had given Mary when the two were kids; she had never gotten it back. Eldredge also had Mary's prom picture in his folder. My family had only a handful of pictures of Mary, and here was this stranger with her only prom picture! I swallowed my anger and asked him to let me hear Albert DeSalvo in his own words.

16 : The Confession

"O kay, I'll let you listen to them," Eldredge said. "But if you ever believed that DeSalvo was *not* the Boston Strangler, these tapes are gonna change your mind."

Eldredge's words disturbed me. Could all my work have been for nothing? Had Albert DeSalvo really murdered my aunt, after all?

We set up another meeting, this time at Eldredge's lawyer's office. I wanted to go alone, but my attorney Elaine Whitfield Sharp insisted on going with me. "If I'm going to represent the families in this case, I must be privy to everything," she said. How could I argue? Eldredge was less than pleased by her presence and said he wouldn't play the tapes unless she waited in the car. After a good deal of pleading by Eldredge's lawyer, Elaine obliged, rolling her eyes at me as she went out.

"You can't be too careful!" Eldredge explained.

When Eldredge pressed "play" on the recorder, I took a deep breath and listened intently to DeSalvo's nasal voice as he described how he had murdered Mary Sullivan. There were two other men in the room with DeSalvo during the taping: John Bottomly and DeSalvo's legal guardian, George McGrath.

BOTTOMLY: The scarf . . . how did you use it?

DESALVO: I tied her up with it.

BOTTOMLY: In what fashion did you tie her? Did you tie her legs too?

DESALVO: This thing has a lot of colors in it, very dark colors.

BOTTOMLY: What did you use it for?

DESALVO: Ah . . . tying of her hands.

BOTTOMLY: The tying of her hands. You had her hands tied in front of her? She still had her clothes on?

DESALVO: Yes.

MCGRATH: She sitting on her bed or lying on it?

DESALVO: She's lying on the bed.

MCGRATH: On her back?

DESALVO: I also tied her feet.

BOTTOMLY: Okay, I want to review this now. First you put a gag in her mouth, you tied her hands and feet. You put a mustard-colored sweater over her head.

DESALVO: The first thing was to tie her hands. Then I put something in her mouth to stop her from screaming. This is very confusing. She did talk to me and I'm trying to get straight what she said . . . I gotta tell 'em [whispering to himself]. The reason why I did what I did . . . the thing was on her face. She did talk to me. I know she don't have no gag in her mouth. I just tied her hands. She was tied, right, and I got on top of her so she couldn't be in any position to reach up and scratch me. Then . . . I strangled her.

MCGRATH: While she was lying on her back? You got the gag in her mouth now?

DESALVO: No . . .

BOTTOMLY: Did she have her clothes off?

DESALVO: Yup.

BOTTOMLY: Is this before or after you had sex?

DESALVO: After . . . her feet was tied there. And her hands were right here. Her hands, I was sitting on them because she was really fighting viciously. . . . So this [sweater] here I put over her head, it was mustard color.

MCGRATH: Where did you get it?

DESALVO: I got the sweater out of her drawer.

MCGRATH: You get the sweater out of her lower drawer?

DESALVO: It should still be there in the room. There's a reason why the sweater was out there in the open.

MCGRATH: You pulled it out from the bottom drawer, then?

DESALVO: Exactly!

MCGRATH: When did you get her clothes off, Albert? You strangled her with her clothes on and you hadn't penetrated her?

DESALVO: No.

BOTTOMLY: And then you cut her hands loose?

DESALVO: This is what I hate to even talk about. This kills me.

MCGRATH: I know.

DESALVO: I'd just as soon forget this whole thing.

MCGRATH: There are other ways this can be verified.

DESALVO: This is very serious stuff. I did penetrate her. She turned sideways. She was still alive when I had intercourse with her. I had intercourse with her. She's alive, she allowed me to do it to her. And then . . . I came inside her. And then I had taken her blue jeans off and her white panties. And after, I said now I'm gonna tie you up and leave. She was naked then . . . I'm trying to think why . . . It don't make sense now. She had her legs up after I took the panties off her. She didn't want me to do it, but I still did it. She argued. I took 'em off her, and her feet went back . . . like this here. [Rustling sounds in the audiotape suggest De-Salvo is physically imitating Mary's position.] I'm trying to think . . . at what time . . . at what time . . . I remember ripping the clothes open. I know this here.

BOTTOMLY: Is this with the knife?

DESALVO: I started ripping the bra off her. This is very confusing to me. I don't know if I did it after or before or how I tied her up. I do remember putting this thing over her face. I'm almost positive I put a gag in her mouth, but why? It don't make sense. I did have intercourse with her right there. And I did, after I tied her hands . . . I did struggle on top of her.

MCGRATH: This is after you had intercourse with her?

DESALVO: This one . . . this one here . . . on, um . . . Mary Sullivan, was it?

BOTTOMLY: Mary Sullivan. You took her pants off before you tied her feet. Is that correct?

DESALVO: Ah . . . no. That's the gimmick right there. The clothes were cut.

BOTTOMLY: She's got this thing over her head, and she's complaining about the heat. Maybe you get sick of her complaining and decide that she's too much of a problem. You certainly strangled her while this [sweater] was over her head, right? You weren't looking right at her face, were you?

DESALVO: No . . . then I got her in this position here, right? But it could not be so that I strangled her in this position because I know differently. Because she was over here . . . she was in this position here.

MCGRATH: By the headboard?

DESALVO: Her knees were crossed, and then I got on top of her . . . and that . . . that's about it.

BOTTOMLY: This is after you had intercourse?

DESALVO: This is what's messin' me up.

BOTTOMLY: Did you have intercourse with her?

DESALVO: Yes, I did . . . but I'll be honest with ya . . .

MCGRATH: Did you come inside her?

DESALVO: Yes, I did. I was so mixed up at the time, but I do remember that I strangled her with my two hands.

MCGRATH: Face to face.

DESALVO: Well, when you say face to face . . .

MCGRATH: She was facing you, you had a sweater over her head.

DESALVO: Yes, I couldn't see her.

MCGRATH: And you strangled her by using your thumbs against her Adam's apple, right? With your thumb?

DESALVO: Yes.

Nick Eldredge stopped the tape and smiled at me. "See, what did I tell you? DeSalvo did it!" Eldredge jumped out of his chair, squeezing his large hands around an invisible victim. "You see how he described killing her?"

I had other thoughts about the tape. Albert DeSalvo claimed he had strangled Mary with his bare hands. But, in fact, she was strangled with two scarves and a nylon stocking. Her autopsy report showed no sign of manual strangulation. DeSalvo also claimed to have had intercourse with my aunt and ejaculated inside her. He says this not just once but twice. But the autopsy report showed no trace of seminal evidence inside the vagina. DeSalvo's using language such as "this one . . . this one here" suggests that he was pointing to or referring to crime scene pictures as he described how Mary's body had been left. To me the conclusion was clear. DeSalvo had gotten the details of Mary's murder completely wrong. This tape was key evidence in our case. I was more certain than ever that DeSalvo had not killed my aunt.

17 : Turning Up the Heat

After hearing the confession tape, I was more determined than ever to push ahead. In May 2000, we held a news conference to lay out our goals and introduce Professor James Starrs to the public. For the event, I chose an oak-paneled room at the elegant Omni Parker House in downtown Boston. It was the same room where John F. Kennedy had announced his first run for Congress. On this day, for the first time, the public would see relatives of the alleged killer and relatives of his alleged victim standing side by side in a common cause.

Elaine Whitfield Sharp began the event by welcoming my mother to the podium. I was nervous for her—Mom had never spoken in front of a large crowd before—but her words were effective. They came from the heart. "This started as a simple request," she said. "Instead, it keeps getting bigger, with denials and cover-ups of a thirty-six-year-old case. Why . . . why don't they want to reopen this case?" Mom asked.

Richard DeSalvo and his son, Tim, were both clearly

nervous about going public for the first time, but Tim, who did the talking for both of them, did not disappoint us. "No one knows the facts," Tim said. "We're hopeful that science will reveal those facts. Let science proceed and let the chips fall where they may."

I went next. I was even more confident than Tim that his uncle was innocent of these crimes. I told reporters that Albert DeSalvo's confession tape, the very thing that connected him to the murders, could also exonerate him. I also used the occasion to put more heat on the attorney general and the Boston Police Department. "It's time for the blue wall of silence to finally be broken in this case," I said from the podium.

The last to speak was Jim Starrs, who had flown up that morning from Washington. He wore a tweed coat with a small pin bearing the emblem of George Washington University. Starrs told the journalists that he had no preconceptions about Albert DeSalvo's guilt or innocence. Science was an impartial judge, he said. Then both Starrs and Elaine Whitfield Sharp asked for more cooperation from Attorney General Tom Reilly and Police Commissioner Paul Evans. None of us wished to exhume the bodies of my aunt or Albert DeSalvo if the evidence was already in possession of the authorities.

Following our news conference, the press immediately went to the attorney general and Boston Police Department for comment. On the steps of the Massachusetts statehouse, Tom Reilly said he was inclined to provide the families access to the case files. If Reilly decided to follow through, he would not be setting a precedent because his predecessor, Scott Harshbarger, had let journalists comb through the strangler files while he was attorney general.

Reaction from the Boston Police Department was much different. In a press release, the BPD said that because of "the deterioration of evidence," the department would not take part in any further investigation into the Boston Strangler case.

Then, a few weeks after Reilly told reporters that he was inclined to cooperate with the families, our lawyers received a letter stating that our request for access to the evidence had been denied. But it was too late to stop us. Through my lobbying efforts, the Boston City Council adopted a resolution calling for a reinvestigation of my aunt's murder. I was also busy getting information about Mary's grave to Jim Starrs. Through the funeral parlor, I learned that Mary had been embalmed and buried in a wooden coffin inside a vault. Starrs was pleased with the news of the embalming because it increased the likelihood that her tissues would be preserved.

While I was hounding the people at the Doane, Beal, and Ames funeral home, I was also keeping close tabs on Nick Eldredge. The public had heard enough from the families; it was time for people to hear from Albert DeSalvo himself. I wanted to release the confession tape to the media. Eldredge had other plans, however. He still hoped to sell the tape. But Eldredge helped me in another way, by telling me about another investigator who had evidence about my aunt's murder. This was Andy Tuney, the Boston Strangler Task Force member who had quit the state police to work for F. Lee Bailey. I called Tuney and asked if he had any information or evidence that could lead me to my aunt's killer.

"You're aunt's killer is dead. He was stabbed to death in prison. He's Albert DeSalvo!" Tuney shouted angrily into the phone.

When I asked him about the mistakes DeSalvo had made in his confession, Tuney had no answer. Then I asked him if working for DeSalvo's defense attorney after having worked for the Boston Strangler Task Force represented a conflict of interest for him. "Lee Bailey and I never talked about the case," he replied. Changing the subject, I asked Tuney whether he had ever searched for other possible suspects, such as Mary's boyfriend Nathan Ward, or Preston Moss, or even DeSalvo's former confidant, George Nassar. "Aw, we checked Nassar's employment records. He was working at the time of the murders. He had a sales job at Filene's," Tuney replied gruffly.

This detail intrigued me. Mary had also worked at Filene's. I had never been able to make a connection between Nassar and my aunt until now. I had to locate the convicted killer George Nassar.

I knew that Nassar had always shied away from reporters when it came to the Boston Strangler case. It was a long shot, but I wrote him a letter requesting a meeting at his current residence, the state prison at Walpole. I was surprised to receive a reply a few days later. I was even more surprised that Nassar wanted to see me. When I went back to the newsroom and told Ted Wayman that Nassar was willing to sit down with me, the veteran reporter John Henning overheard our conversation.

"Be careful," warned Henning, who had covered De-Salvo's Green Man trial in 1967. "George Nassar is a cold son of a bitch. He's a pathological liar, and he'd kill you just as soon as look at you."

Laura and my mother were also worried. "Don't give him any personal information," Laura advised. She was now seven months pregnant. I lied and said that as a journalist I dealt with dangerous characters all the time. Deep inside, I felt frightened, but I needed to look into Nassar's eyes and ask him if he had murdered Mary. I had heard that Nassar was suffering from terminal cancer. Maybe Nassar was ready to give me a deathbed confession.

Elaine Sharp advised me not to tackle Nassar head-on but to elicit any information I could in a more roundabout way. "Why would Nassar agree to do an interview?" she wondered. "There has to be something in it for him. Guards go through all the mail, and maybe your letter piqued some interest. Maybe word has gotten back to Tom Reilly about what you're doing." She took a moment and laughed off her last comment, adding, "It's possible that one day we'll benefit from my paranoia."

On the day of the interview I awoke early to prepare myself, allowing a few bites of a bagel to float around with the butterflies in my stomach. Then, pouring a hot cup of black coffee to go, I hopped into my car and began the hour-long drive to Walpole. Again, I called on Mary to give me the strength I needed to get through this.

Arriving in Walpole, I couldn't find the prison. There were no signs pointing the way to it, either. Apparently, residents didn't want to remind themselves or inform others that they had the worst criminals in Massachusetts for neighbors. Even when I asked for directions, the townsfolk gave me little help.

Eventually, atop a steep hill I noticed a small sign for the state penitentiary. Dark clouds took shape as I made my way up the long stretch of road to the prison. The unsettled weather gave the ominous structure an even more sinister appearance.

Inside the prison, I filled out the customary visitor form, which asked for my name and address, and whether the visit was personal or for business. I checked off business, but for me it was really both. After I turned in my completed form, a guard told me I could not take my notepad or pen with me into the visiting area. All personal belongings, including my watch, had to stay on the outside.

At 9:50 A.M., I was called out of the visitors' waiting room and told to walk through a large steel door. Once through it, I was ordered to take off my shoes and belt, empty my pockets, and then walk through a metal detector. Past the metal detector, my anxiety building, I proceeded through another steel door and into a small and barren courtyard. I was now inside the most frightening place in New England. I was also just moments away from meeting a man whom I knew only from a thirty-five-year-old photograph, a man with the cold eyes of a cobra.

"You here to see Nassar?" a muscular guard asked. "Room five!" he barked before I had time to answer.

Room five wasn't a room at all but a small cubicle with two metal chairs and two phones on either side of a dirty reinforced glass partition. I stared through the glass and watched as the door on the other side opened electronically. In walked a tall, thin man with salt-and-pepper hair. Nassar's cheeks were hollow, his once-olive skin now a dull gray. His eyes, however, were exactly as I'd remembered them from the photograph: lifeless.

Nassar slowly walked toward his side of the cubicle, sat down, and picked up the phone. Neither one of us said anything at first. We just sat there. The cobra was trying to hypnotize its prey. My gaze left his and I focused on his hands. They were bony yet powerful-looking.

"I know what you're thinking," he hissed. "You think you're looking at Hannibal Lecter, don't you?" Nassar was referring to the fictional serial killer from *The Silence of the Lambs*.

"No . . . I'm just looking at a tired old man who's gonna die in prison!" I replied. I don't know where the line came from, but it sounded tough.

Nassar cracked a smile. It was a collage of decaying teeth, the result of decades of neglect. "So what can I do for you, Mr. Sherman?"

"You know why I'm here. I want to talk about the Boston Strangler case." I took a deep breath. "Are you the Boston Strangler, and did you kill my aunt?"

"I never killed anybody. Anybody!" Nassar shouted.

I was starting to see the wisdom of Elaine's advice about getting information in a roundabout way. I'd have to come back to that question. I asked Nassar about his relationship with Albert DeSalvo.

"We met at Bridgewater," he said, "after a friend of mine told me about him. He said DeSalvo was saying crazy things about killing women."

"Did he discuss the murders with you?" I asked.

"He tried to, especially about the Samans murder. But I have a weak stomach for that kind of stuff. I don't like to talk about the macabre," replied Nassar, a man who had gunned down a gas station attendant in cold blood while the victim pleaded for his life.

"You know, there are a lot of people out there who say that you really killed those women," I said, trying to bait him.

Nassar looked me right in the eyes. "What do you think?"

"Well, I've heard the confession tape, and I know it wasn't DeSalvo," I said. "I spoke with Andy Tuney, and he told me that you were working at Filene's at the time of the murders. Is that true?"

Nassar shook his head. "I was working at Raymond's Department Store, near Jordan Marsh."

My hope that I was confronting Mary's killer was starting to fade. Raymond's Department Store had been near Filene's, and Nassar and Mary could have crossed paths, but the connection would have been much stronger if the two had been coworkers.

"Did you ever spend time on Beacon Hill?" I asked.

"No, I was working most of the time. Beacon Hill wasn't exactly my crowd," he answered matter-of-factly.

Switching gears, I started quizzing him about the fatal stabbing of Albert DeSalvo. I asked Nassar if he knew DeSalvo was planning to tell what he called "the real story" of the Boston Strangler.

"Al told me the week before that he was going to call Ames Robey, but I advised against it," Nassar said. "Al always liked to play games with Robey, and I didn't know what Robey's take on this whole thing was."

"Why was DeSalvo killed?" I asked.

"Al was killed over a petty argument with another inmate. I think it was over a slab of bacon. Al was getting high a lot, too."

"So you didn't kill him or have him killed because he was going to pin the murders on you?"

"I didn't have a hand in that, no. Al's mouth always got him in trouble."

I could sense Nassar was lying about his possible role in DeSalvo's murder. If he had committed any of the stranglings, Nassar would have much to lose by De-Salvo's revelation that he was not the Boston Strangler. Yes, Nassar was serving a life sentence for murder, but he had attempted several times to get a new trial. George Nassar had not given up on freedom. I was able to get out of him the facts that he knew of DeSalvo's plan to expose the truth and that Nassar had been close friends with Vinny "The Bear" Flemmi, the underworld hit man some believe committed the murder. Would prison guards have looked the other way if DeSalvo was killed over a slab of bacon? Nassar ended by telling me that his cancer was in remission. "Gee, George, that's too bad," I said to him as I called the guard to let me out.

18 : Twists and Turns

Was George Nassar a cold-blooded killer? Absolutely. Did he kill Mary Sullivan? A good journalist follows the evidence wherever it leads, and there was no tangible evidence to point to Nassar's guilt in the murder of my aunt. The list of possible suspects was getting smaller. Meanwhile, Massachusetts authorities were insisting that despite an exhaustive search, they could not find any physical evidence from Mary's murder. My mother and I had hoped things would never get to the point where we would really have to think about exhuming Mary's body. We thought that the attorney general eventually would give us the evidence we needed to pursue the case. But by late summer 2000, there was no movement by Tom Reilly or anyone else in law enforcement. Reilly was calling our bluff.

We could continue to beg for the evidence the state claimed did not exist or we could attempt to solve Mary's murder on our own. And to do it on our own, we would have to exhume Mary's remains. It was a painful decision for Mom, a devout Catholic who did not want to go against her religion by desecrating her sister's grave. Mom was also feeling pressure from within her own family. Her brother and sisters were not eager to see the case reopened. Mom felt Mary's presence strongly as she agonized over a decision. She believed that Mary wanted us to pursue the case and that Mary would lead us to her killer. Professor Starrs made another trip north to take soil samples from St. Francis Xavier Cemetery, where Mary was buried. Starrs paid his own way to Cape Cod and back, never asking for any money from my mother or me. "This project must be pro bono," he insisted. "I do not want anyone to think my forensic team is beholden to the families in any way. The results of our investigation will not be compromised."

Elaine and Dan Sharp were also offering their help free of charge, working countless hours preparing legal briefs for what appeared to be the long court battle ahead. If we had had to pay for it, this reinvestigation of Mary's murder would have cost us a half million dollars.

Meanwhile, however, people were talking about the Boston Strangler case for the first time in nearly forty years. Because I was spearheading the reinvestigation, much of the attention focused on me. I had always worked behind the scenes in television news, so for me this was daunting. Not only were we getting requests for television interviews, but I also started to receive strange phone calls at home. The first came late at night. Laura now was only weeks away from delivery, and she'd been going to sleep much earlier than usual. I would spend those nights sitting on the living room couch with my furry companion, Bailey, contemplating fatherhood and thinking about the case.

One of these nights, the telephone rang. I thought it was probably my brother calling from California. Todd had been living on the West Coast for ten years but still hadn't quite grasped the three-hour time difference. I reached for the phone and said, "Hello?" I got no response. "Who is this?" I asked, but again nothing. Finally, I heard a voice: "You're causing a lot of problems. This isn't ancient history. There's a lot of people who could get hurt by you digging around in the past."

"Who is this?" I asked.

"Leave it alone," the voice said. Then the line went dead.

I immediately punched in *69, hoping to trace the call, but all I got was a recorded message telling me the call had originated from a number that was out of the area or unpublished. I then called my best friend, Toby, who liked to play practical jokes, but his answering machine said he was out of town on business. Next, I went around the house, making sure every door was locked. I grabbed a hammer from the closet, held it tightly in my hand, and waited for an intruder. In time, Bailey and I fell asleep on the couch.

I didn't tell Laura what had happened. The doctor had just put her on bed rest for the last two weeks of her pregnancy, and I didn't want to add to her stress. I made plans to change our phone number, but before I could do that, I received another call. This time, the caller wasn't a deep-voiced man, however; she was a soft-spoken older woman. "I just wanted to let you know that what you're doing is wonderful," she told me. "You see, my aunt was also killed by the Boston Strangler, and my family never believed DeSalvo was the real murderer." The caller was the niece of the second Boston Strangler victim, Nina

Nichols. I thanked her for her kind words and asked if she would be willing to join us in our quest for the truth.

"If I were a bit younger," she replied. "But my husband and I are old, and we're tired. We've seen the problems you've faced. We can't go through that. But I do wish you the best of luck for your aunt's sake, and for mine."

Though this caller did not join our team, she inspired me to push on. I had abandoned trying to contact the relatives of other Boston Strangler victims. Most of the victims had been elderly, and the younger victims often were college students transplanted from other parts of the country. But my caller reminded me that there were other relatives out there who did not believe the official version of the Boston Strangler case and were watching our struggle closely.

A few days later, I tracked down the son of a Boston Strangler victim whom, for reasons of privacy, I will not identify here. I called him at his office and asked if he knew about the reinvestigation into the Boston Strangler case. He told me he had read something about it in the *Boston Globe*.

I didn't want to dredge up painful feelings for him, but I felt I had to let him know what was going on. I said, "I don't know how much you know about your mother's murder, but my family believes that Albert DeSalvo was not the killer and that the real killers are still out there. I would appreciate any support you could give me in finding the truth about what happened."

"Well, Mr. Sherman, I do believe they got the right fellow, and I do believe that justice was done," he replied.

I could have debated the merits of the case with him,

but it appeared to me that this guy's mind was made up. After the conversation, I called Jim Mellon.

"Jim, I'm kinda surprised, but the son is convinced that DeSalvo was the guy. He really believes it."

"No, he doesn't," Mellon replied matter-of-factly.

"Why do you say that?"

"Because we always believed he killed his mother." Mellon told me that investigators had been suspicious of the son from the beginning. The young man had been undergoing psychiatric treatment, and Mellon interviewed his therapist. "What took you so long?" the psychiatrist asked Mellon. "Do I think he did it?" the shrink asked rhetorically. "Yup! Will I testify to it? No fucking way."

Mellon knew he had the killer, but he also knew he didn't have a case without the therapist's testimony. But the shrink vowed never to break the confidentiality agreement between doctor and patient.

In late July 2000, my wife gave birth to our daughter, Isabella. With late-night feedings, I was getting little sleep. While I took up the role of first-time dad, Jim Starrs was selecting his exhumation team, and the Sharps were hard at work drafting papers for the lawsuits. Their Marblehead office, now the unofficial headquarters for the strangler reinvestigation, had very little space to walk around; piles of files seemed to be everywhere. The case, which Elaine Sharp had dubbed the Mary and Albert Project, was expanding in size and scope. The Sharps were filing five suits, one against each of the bureaus involved in the original investigation. The attorneys were preparing to argue that items belonging to Mary and to Albert DeSalvo should be returned to their rightful heirs, an argument used successfully in Native Americans' legal battles over tribal land taken from their ancestors. Dan Sharp was cautiously optimistic that the case could be won. "It all depends on the judge," Dan said. "The government is the worst possible opponent to go after because they can bury you in paperwork, and they have endless funds to boot. But with the right judge, one who won't kiss the government's ass, anything is possible."

We decided to hold a second news conference, this time to announce the lawsuits. The media had been our most effective weapon against the government thus far. On September 14, 2000, reporters and television trucks gathered early at the Royal Sonesta Hotel in Cambridge. This time, the story would receive national coverage from *CBS Evening News*. Again, my mother and I stood side by side with the DeSalvo family at the podium. Elaine Sharp began by laying the blame at the feet of Attorney General Tom Reilly. "He said publicly that he would grant the family access to the case files," Sharp argued, "but privately he slammed the door in our faces. We are not looking for money; we are looking for the truth." After she was finished, the DeSalvos and my mother spoke about their need for closure. But the day's most startling words came not from the lawyers or the families but from Albert DeSalvo himself. It was time to release DeSalvo's confession tape to the world. The reporters made a small circle around a television monitor in the corner of the conference room. Nick Eldredge had finally allowed me to make a copy of DeSalvo's taped confession to my aunt's murder. To enhance the sound quality, I had transferred my tiny audiocassette to video the night before. Elaine Sharp handed out copies of Mary's autopsy report for the media to compare with DeSalvo's taped words. Reporters started pushing and shoving, some using their microphones as weapons to get the best possible spot by the television screen. "This is the tape that the government doesn't want you to hear," I said. Then I pressed the Play button.

For the first time, reporters heard DeSalvo's description of Mary Sullivan's murder. And for the first time, they were given undeniable proof that Albert DeSalvo was fabricating his story. They heard DeSalvo say he had choked Mary by pressing his thumbs against her Adam's apple. The reporters leafed through the autopsy report and saw that Mary had not been manually strangled. They also heard DeSalvo say he ejaculated inside my aunt's body. Elaine and I pointed out the paragraph in the autopsy report that stated that no trace of semen had been found in Mary's vagina. Reporters began to smile and nod. They knew there was more to this story than they had first believed.

Later that day, I received a telephone call from a producer at the *CBS Early Show* featuring Bryant Gumbel. She asked if I would appear on the program live, opposite F. Lee Bailey. It was a moment I had dreamed about, but I was nervous. Before I agreed to appear on the show, I called Elaine and Dan. I pointed out that they were more qualified to discuss the legal issues of the case. "Yes, but it will be more effective coming from you," Elaine advised. "Don't worry, you'll be fine."

The interview was done via satellite from the WBZ newsroom. I arrived early that morning to prepare. I knew I would be facing one of the most celebrated and reviled lawyers of the twentieth century. There was a good chance I would be eaten alive. "Just stick to the facts," I told myself over and over. "Despite what Bailey says, the facts of the case will speak for themselves." Members of the WBZ production crew sat me down in the studio and handed me an earpiece. I could hear the *Early Show* producers giving Gumbel his cues in New York. Then I was asked to stare straight into the camera. I could not see Gumbel or, more important, F. Lee Bailey, who was talking via satellite from Palm Beach, Florida.

The first question was to me. "What's the point of all this? Why now?" Gumbel asked, a trace of annoyance in his voice.

"Well, Bryant, my family doesn't believe Albert De-Salvo was the Boston Strangler, and we're here to find her killer," I replied.

Gumbel, who clearly had not done his homework, countered that all the investigators agreed they had gotten the right man.

"Some of the investigators are saying that, and that's because these people don't care about truth, they don't care about justice. What they care about is how they'll be remembered when they're gone, and they all want to be remembered as the men who caught the Boston Strangler, and that's simply not true," I replied, my jitters now gone.

Gumbel then went to Bailey, who, when I was able to view the tape later on, looked as if he had just rolled out of bed for the interview. His face was bloated, his suit was rumpled, and he sat hunched over in his chair. "I think this is a lot of hogwash. The young man wasn't even alive when this happened," Bailey said. "Albert said he had intercourse with her, and that's all he said." I tried to correct him, but the legendary lawyer cut me off. Bailey might still have been shaking off the cobwebs, but he knew that this television segment could last only a short time. He was doing his best to filibuster his way through it. "There was no room for questioning when people like

Andy Tuney and Ed Brooke were done. Albert was the Boston Strangler," Bailey insisted.

This time, Bailey was cut off, by Bryant Gumbel. "Mr. Sherman, what do you have to say to this?"

"Albert DeSalvo said he had sex with my aunt; he said he ejaculated inside my aunt. This was disproved by the official autopsy report. Albert DeSalvo was completely wrong, and, Mr. Bailey, so are you!"

For a few awkward moments, F. Lee Bailey was speechless. Gumbel called for a commercial, and I walked out into the newsroom to a standing ovation from my colleagues. I felt like David slaying Goliath, but I also knew we had a long way to go.

19 : The Exhumation

While the media were focused on our lawsuits, final plans were secretly being made for Mary's exhumation. My mother did not want this to become a media event, and Jim Starrs assured us that it would be done quickly and quietly. Mom went to the Barnstable town hall and picked up the proper permits. Starrs had lengthy conversations with the caretaker of St. Francis Xavier Cemetery, who was intrigued by the idea. The owners of the nearby John Lawrence Funeral Home offered to donate their facilities for Mary's new autopsy. Everyone involved in the project was sworn to secrecy. After denying several requests, we finally relented and allowed a camera crew from the CBS news program *48 Hours* to film at the cemetery. The network news program, which was working on an hour-long special on the case, had pressed us hard about attending the exhumation. Having weighed the pros and cons, we decided that the media were vital to our success. Even my mother went along, though she wasn't especially happy about it. Mom realized that the program was not going to air for several months, and she hoped the pain involved in approving the exhumation would not be as fresh then.

Jim Starrs and his team arrived on Cape Cod on Friday, October 13, 2000. Starrs wanted to open Mary's grave the day before the exhumation to determine what condition her remains were in. Members of the group delicately dug up the area around the tombstone, making a conscious effort not to disturb the other caskets in the family plot, which contained the remains of my Grandmother Florry, my Grandfather Jack, and my Uncle David, who had died suddenly of a heart attack in 1995. When the team reached Mary's casket, Starrs was disappointed to discover that the cover had caved in and the casket was filled with water. Starrs gave this information to Elaine Sharp, who broke the news to my mother later that evening back at Sharp's hotel. Trembling, Mom told her a story that she had told me a few years before. "I remember sitting at my kitchen table and I heard a voice coming from the hall," she said. "At first, I thought it was the television set, but then I remembered that the TV wasn't on. The voice was very familiar to me. I went into the hall to see what the noise was, and I saw my sister. Mary was standing right in front of me. She was saying, 'Find my killer, find my killer.' Mary was wearing a white nightgown, and she was soaking wet. Her hair was wet, and her clothes were wet. I didn't know why she was wet. It has bothered me for years. But now I know why."

I drove to Cape Cod the next morning. The fog of early dawn had lifted, replaced by brilliant sun and balmy temperatures. I got to the cemetery just before nine. Starrs and his team were already gathered. Starrs's spirits were high, thanks to the arrival of his friend and colleague Dr. Michael Baden, the former chief medical examiner in New York City. Baden had testified in the O. J. Simpson trial and had his own television program on forensic science on HBO. He was a mountain of a man with wild, curly hair and a thick mustache, but his physical appearance belied a caring nature. He told me in a soft voice that he sincerely hoped the work done on this day would lead to closure for my family. "Your mother is a very brave woman. She cares deeply for her sister and we will not let her down," he said.

Mom didn't come to the cemetery for the exhumation. Instead, she wanted to spend the beautiful Indian summer day walking Sea Street Beach, thinking about her sister. Mary was not at the graveyard, Mom told herself, but alive at her favorite spot in the world, the beach. I attended the exhumation in Mom's place. Since I had never known Mary, I thought I could observe the exhumation and keep my emotions in check. I was wrong. When I saw the scientists lifting the casket out of the ground, my eyes welled up with tears, and I could barely breathe. Once again I wondered about the wisdom of exhuming Mary's body. Then Starrs walked up to me with a quizzical look. "We found another set of remains at the foot of your aunt's grave. They are the remains of an infant," he said. I had to look away. The casket Starrs had found, I knew, held the remains of my sister, Susan, born two years after me. She had been stillborn, and my mother had her laid to rest next to Mary, so that Mary could watch over her. I thanked God that Mom wasn't there.

Out of respect for my aunt's memory and for their surroundings, Starrs's team of scientists spoke in hushed tones throughout the unearthing of Mary's body. Elaine Sharp took copious notes and pictures that she hoped would one day be presented to a jury. "She'll lead us to her killer, I really believe that," Elaine said, giving me a hug as we watched the scientists carefully place Mary's remains into a waiting hearse.

I followed the caravan of vehicles from the cemetery to the funeral parlor. It was like a funeral procession, but in reverse.

I declined an invitation to observe the autopsy. Instead, I sat upstairs in the funeral parlor, awaiting word from Baden and Starrs. I wanted to remember Mary as she was in her high school yearbook picture, young and smiling.

Now it was time for Michael Baden to go to work. The first thing the scientists noticed when they placed the remains on the table was that Mary was still holding rosary beads. They spent the next several hours examining Mary's remains for possible trace evidence of her killer. First, they ran an ultraviolet light over her body, hoping to find signs of seminal fluid. Baden and the crew also took swabs of Mary's mouth and vaginal area. The work would continue into early evening. In all, the scientists extracted over sixty biological samples for later testing.

The team members got together later that evening for dinner at Barbyann's, a Hyannis steak house. Starrs, who was putting the team up in hotel rooms with money from his own pocket, said he'd also pay for dinner. My mother and I protested, but the professor wouldn't hear of our paying. Starrs was once again wearing his tweed coat, but this time he was also carrying a wool sock that contained a can of Guinness—mother's milk, according to Starrs. "What is the sock for?" I asked. He looked at me as if my question was absurd. "To keep it warm, of course," he said.

As the night progressed the drinks flowed, and Starrs and Michael Baden began discussing the idea of holding a news conference the next day. This was exactly what my mother and I didn't want. Mom was already uncomfortable over the fact that television cameras had filmed the exhumation. Although the *48 Hours* special would not air for months, our emotions were still raw at this time and we didn't want to be forced to share that with an audience. Knowing we were upset, Sharp said, "The story will get out; it always does. Let Jim hold the news conference and get ahead of the story before the story gets ahead of us."

The next day, Starrs announced that we had exhumed Mary's body, and reporters from Boston rushed to the Cape for the news conference. There Starrs and Baden discussed the purpose of the exhumation, and Sharp once again emphasized the need for cooperation from the government. I reminded reporters that this was by no means a fruitless exercise. "We are not chasing ghosts here. The real killers of these women are still out there," I said.

Later that afternoon, Mary was laid to rest once again. My mother's new husband, Ken Dodd, had built Mary a new casket that my mother-in-law, Ann, lined with Irish linen. Instead of jetting out of town with their forensic evidence, Jim Starrs and his team attended the reburial, serving as pallbearers. Again, the sun shone brilliantly. A Catholic priest offered a prayer as Mary's remains were returned to the ground. "It was beautiful. It was the way Mary's first funeral should have been, quiet and dignified," my mother said afterward. I had feared the weekend would be traumatic for her, but it had turned out quite the opposite. "It was like I had my sister back," she said, "if only for a couple of days."

The exhumation made news around the world. The *Times* of London reported it, as did the *Daily Scotsman,* and I got interview requests from as far away as South Korea. I explained to the foreign journalists that my mother had been forced into the exhumation because authorities in Massachusetts said there was no physical evidence left in my aunt's murder case. The exhumation was our best hope of finding out who the killer was.

One morning soon after the exhumation, I groggily walked out to my driveway to fetch the newspapers. The weather had gotten cold again, and my golden retriever refused to go outside to do the chore herself. Back inside, I took my first sip of coffee. The first section of the *Boston Globe* did not hold my interest, so I turned to the Metro section, where a column by Brian McGrory caught my eye. According to McGrory, Attorney General Tom Reilly had recently turned up evidence of semen from Mary's murder. I nearly spit out my coffee. McGrory, who had once called Reilly a "French poodle" for his less than vigilant approach to this case, was now praising him for digging through dusty basements in search of evidence. "What a load of bullshit!" I screamed. I knew that Reilly had been lying to us when he claimed such evidence did not exist. He had had it all along but hoped that the families would go away. And what timing! If the attorney general's office had told us about the seminal evidence, we would never have gone through with the exhumation. To top it all off, Reilly had told McGrory that he was reopening the Mary Sullivan case, yet he had never even bothered to tell her family. My mother was being victimized once again.

I forced myself to sit back and think about what was best for the case. Maybe his comments to McGrory were

Reilly's subtle way of extending the olive branch. Swallowing my pride, I phoned his office and was granted another meeting.

This time, we were well represented by Elaine and Dan Sharp. "Leone thinks he's still in the marines," Dan said as we rode the elevator to the eighteenth floor. "He has a procedure for everything. Getting him to think creatively on this could be impossible."

Leone did not offer his hand to me as we entered the small conference room; he merely guided us toward the empty chairs. Next to Leone sat a young woman who did not introduce herself. We all assumed she was Leone's aide.

"We're here to make a deal," Dan announced. "You seem to have something we want, and we seem to have something you want."

Elaine broke in. "We will suspend our lawsuit today if we can have an assurance that any forensic testing done in this case will be done aboveboard and not under a veil of secrecy."

"What do you mean by that?" Leone asked.

"Professor Jim Starrs has sent you a letter," Elaine advised. Before Leone could say he hadn't received it, Elaine slid a copy of it under his palm. "Professor Starrs is offering any and all information he and his team discover in their forensic reinvestigation of Mary Sullivan's murder. Now in response, Diane and Casey would like Starrs to be involved in any DNA testing done in your state labs," Elaine said.

Leone sat back in his seat, staring at the four of us. "Now, Elaine, this is a homicide investigation, and we do not solicit any outside help. It could jeopardize the case."

Now it was Dan's turn. "We're not asking that Starrs

do the actual testing. We're asking that he be allowed to observe. You know, the guy's done this type of work before. He may actually be able to help you. He'd even sign a confidentiality agreement so as to not tell the families what you've found."

"Any DNA testing done in the Mary Sullivan case will be done by state investigators. And if we need the information Starrs and his team come up with, we'll get it," Leone warned.

The legal sparring continued for several more minutes. Finally, my mother had had enough. "We come up here again and again, and you still tell us no. The best people in the world are working on Mary's murder, and you say that you don't need their help," she said, her voice cracking.

Leone told her involving outsiders in a state investigation simply wasn't the way things were done.

I reached out for my mother's hand, but my eyes were focused on Leone's. "So that's it, then," I stated. "We'll continue with our private and successful investigation, and you can continue to do whatever it is that you do here."

"Looks like we'll see you in court, Gerry," Dan added with a smile as we all got up to leave.

Then my mother turned to the woman who had been sitting quietly next to Leone for the entire meeting. "I'm sorry, miss, but who are you?" Mom asked.

"I'm your victim's advocate. I work as your liaison with the attorney general's office. I'm working for you," the woman replied.

"Then what the hell are you doing sitting next to him?" Mom asked, pointing toward Leone. Before the woman could answer, we were out in the hallway, walking toward the elevator.

*   *   *

"All rise!" the bailiff ordered as Chief U.S. District Judge William G. Young entered the courtroom on February 21, 2001. My mother and I watched from a crowded gallery. Behind us, Dan Sharp stood alone at one table, while five lawyers representing the state of Massachusetts and the Boston Police Department stood at the other. Judge Young was hearing our motion to block the state from conducting further DNA tests on evidence found at Mary's crime scene. The Sharps had recently discovered that the attorney general was in possession of six semen samples taken from Mary's body. Her killer, it turned out, had ejaculated on her chest, not inside her vagina, the way DeSalvo had claimed. The samples, which had been placed on slides in 1964, were reportedly hidden away in a vault at the state medical examiner's office. The morning of the court hearing, Tom Reilly had told reporters that DNA testing in the Sullivan case had been "nonproductive" up to this point. "We are continuing our efforts to analyze that evidence to see if it can be probed. Whether or not it will be, I can't answer that," Reilly told the *Boston Herald*.

Our worst fears had been realized. Tom Reilly was burning the evidence—literally. In the process of DNA testing, scientists must burn the material to obtain a genetic sequence. As a result, once a DNA sample is tested, it can never be tested again. We were not worried that Reilly's DNA testing would place Albert DeSalvo at the scene of the crime but that the test results would come back conveniently "inconclusive."

"The defendants are in the process of destroying evidence even as we speak," Dan warned the judge. Judge Young then called Tom Reilly's legal representative, Judith Kalman, to the floor. "It's been thirty-six years,"

Judge Young began. "Why can't you share the evidence you have? What could it hurt?"

Kalman told Young that Mary Sullivan's murder was an open and active case and that any sharing of the evidence would jeopardize a future prosecution. But how "open and active" was the state's case? What Judge Young did not know was that the attorney general's office had yet to question any key witnesses in the case. I knew my mother and I had not been consulted, and Jim Mellon was still sitting in his seaside home, waiting for a phone call.

Despite the plea from the Sharps, the judge refused to halt the state's DNA testing, but he did get the state to promise to leave enough DNA evidence for the families to conduct an independent test should we win our case. Judge Young, who appeared particularly concerned with the intense media coverage the case was getting, also slapped a gag order on the lawyers and Jim Starrs. Starrs and his team were in Seattle that day for a conference of forensic scientists, where Starrs had promised a progress report on the team's work in the case. In fact, Elaine Sharp had flown to the West Coast to get Starrs's information firsthand. Not surprisingly, the judge's order did not sit well with the professor. "Science needs to be conducted out in the open," Starrs argued. But there would be no progress report that night. The families, however, were not bound by the judge's gag order. I was going to remain on top of this case, pushing and prodding Tom Reilly into doing the right thing.

Judge Young gave one final order that day: he ordered both sides to be back in court the next week so that he could hear the state's request to dismiss our lawsuit. Judge Young, who taught at Harvard Law School, scheduled the hearing for February 27, 2001, inside a lecture hall on the Cambridge campus.

Word that the Boston Strangler case was to be argued on campus spread quickly among Harvard students, and the lecture hall was packed when my mother and I arrived. Richard DeSalvo and members of his family also attended the hearing. While the Sharps were preparing their oral argument, Elaine slipped me a copy of Gerry Leone's affidavit about his work in this case. "Take a look, and tell me what you think," she suggested. I sat down next to Mom, wiped my eyeglasses clean, and began reading.

Leone had written: "On November 19, 1999, I was first notified by First Assistant Attorney General Dean Richlin that he had received a general inquiry regarding the Boston Strangler and whether we had any intention of opening the investigation into those crimes. As a result of that inquiry, throughout the next several months, I gathered all information and materials regarding the cases that were attributed to the Boston Strangler. . . . I became acquainted with the facts of the cases and the then present status of each case. . . . In March 2000, some four months after beginning my search for information, I was first contacted by a person who identified himself as a member of the Mary Sullivan family, Casey Sherman."

Contrary to Leone's affidavit, there had been no "general inquiry" into the Boston Strangler case in November 1999. I had had a direct conversation with the attorney general himself shortly after the WBZ report on Michael DeSalvo aired on November 7, 1999. Leone also got the date of our "first contact" wrong. I had had several discussions with Leone about my aunt's murder dating back to November 1999. The attorney general's office was try-

ing to convince Judge Young that it had been spearheading a probe long before I got involved and that, therefore,
the families had no right to evidence or information about
the case.

During oral arguments of the motion to dismiss, the
Sharps pointed out, as they had done the week before,
that there was no "open or active" criminal investigation
into Mary's murder and argued that the evidence should
therefore be immediately turned over to the families.
Once again, the state argued that any sharing of the evidence would taint any future prosecution. Seeming annoyed, the judge ordered Leone and the Sharps to
negotiate some kind of compromise. The parties went out
into the hallway, where they tried to strike a deal. By then
I had finished reading Leone's affidavit, and I rushed out
into the hallway. "Elaine, I need to speak with you," I
said, interrupting Leone in mid-sentence. "What's up?"
Elaine asked. "Don't believe a word Leone is saying right
now. He doesn't want to share the evidence. Something
very strange is going on here." I pointed out the inaccuracies in Leone's affidavit. "Let's nail him!" I said under
my breath. Elaine glanced back at Leone, who seemed to
be nervous. "Hold that thought," she replied.

At that point, the judge came out in the hall and ordered everyone back in the courtroom, where he asked
the attorneys if the negotiation had been successful. It
had not. Leone still would not budge on our request to
share the semen slides. The state had six in its possession;
we were asking for only one sample. Back in the courtroom, the state's lawyers once again asked the judge to
dismiss our claim, but Judge Young refused to do so. That
our lawsuit remained alive came as a pleasant surprise for
the Sharps, who had worried about the judge's reputation

as a government ally. "Now, that's called kickin' their ass!" Dan Sharp whispered to me as we left the courtroom.

On the courthouse steps, I pulled Elaine aside to discuss the Leone affidavit. "We should point out the inaccuracies in Leone's affidavit," I urged. Elaine clearly had other ideas. "This is much like a poker game," she said. "With that affidavit, we now have a full house. The trick here is not to cash out too early. Let the pot build a while. Let's use that information when we really need it."

It seemed to me that the time to use the information was right now, but I took Elaine's advice, though I believed we were missing a great opportunity to show the world how duplicitous the attorney general's office was.

20 : A Call from New Hampshire

I was always more comfortable behind the camera than in front, but this case needed a spokesman, and the Sharps had chosen me for the job. The public now knew who I was and, more important, how to reach me. Calls flooded the newsroom. I wanted to take every one, no matter how ridiculous, because I couldn't know which one might lead me in the right direction. Most times, I'd field phone calls from drunks with outlandish stories about the "real Boston Strangler." One caller insisted the killer was Senator Ted Kennedy. "Think about it," he slurred. "The Kennedys are responsible for everything."

After calls like this one, I'd have a good laugh and return to the work of producing a TV newscast. But one phone call would change everything. "I don't know if I should be talking to you, but I thought I'd give it a try," the caller said. I hugged the phone receiver to my chin and braced myself for yet another pointless conversation. "I work with a guy who may be involved in your aunt's murder."

"Where are you calling from?" I asked.

"New Hampshire," said the caller. "I work in a bar, and for New Year's our boss took all of the employees out to dinner. The guy I work with brought his wife along. During the course of the evening, the wife started to drink, and then she started to talk. She told me that he was worried about something in his past, something that has to do with the Boston Strangler case. So that's why I called you."

"What's his name?" I asked.

He replied, "His name is Preston Moss."

I told the caller that Moss once was considered the prime suspect in my aunt's murder. "He's always been a real weird guy," the caller told me. "When he first came to New Hampshire, he claimed he was a fighter pilot in Vietnam, and that he rescued POWs. I've known him for about twenty years, but I never really hung around with him." Having researched Moss's background, I knew he'd never served in the military. Still, many people lie about their backgrounds. This didn't mean Moss was a killer. I needed more.

"I'd like to help you; just tell me how," the caller offered.

I told him that by forging a bond with Moss, he might help me find the truth in this case. "Be a friend to Preston," I advised, "and maybe he'll open up about his past."

The caller said he would try. "You know," he told me, "every year, all the folks who work at the bar would head down to Boston to catch a Sox game or to see the Bruins. Every year, the only one who would never go was Preston. Now I understand why."

Immediately after this conversation, I phoned Elaine

Sharp and told her about it. Ever the attorney, she pointed out what we had and what we didn't have against Moss. "Right now, we have opportunity and access. He failed two polygraph exams, so let's assume he stole the keys to get inside Mary's apartment. This theory is also backed up by the fact that there was no forced entry. We have Jim Mellon, who is positive Moss is the guy. Now we have Moss's colleague, who describes a very bizarre conversation with the suspect's wife. But what we still don't have is a motive," she said.

I had been trying to piece together a motive for several months. The caller had told me that Moss had a reputation for being fiercely jealous. Moss's girlfriend at the time, Pat Delmore, had received several letters from a young man in the army stationed in Texas. Those letters were on the list of items taken by the police from Mary's apartment. They also found a receipt for a bus ticket to Texas dated January 1, 1964. So the soldier had possibly visited Delmore just days before the murder.

Now, suppose the fiercely jealous Moss suspected that Delmore was having an affair with this soldier. He needs proof. He steals the apartment key, and when he enters to find those letters, Moss doesn't know that Mary is there, moving things into the apartment. Mary sees him, and he snaps; he loses control, ripping her sweater off and strangling her. This becomes a murder of passion. He sees her naked body and becomes aroused. His sexual frustration is unleashed and he ejaculates on her body. He stands there exhausted, trying to collect his thoughts. Now he's got a dead woman on his hands. He decorates the crime scene, grabbing the broom and the Happy New Year card. He wants the police to believe the murder was the act of the Boston Strangler.

Over the next several weeks, the caller from New Hampshire would check in and recount his conversations with Moss. "He's scared shitless," he told me. "He knows what's goin' on down there." At one point, the caller asked Moss point-blank whether he had killed Mary. Moss did not say yes or no; instead, he stared off into space and said, "I was nineteen. I was nineteen. Why is this all coming back to me now?" The caller then asked him, "What are you worried about? You didn't kill her. It's not your DNA, right?" Moss replied, "They'll sabotage it. That's how my DNA will show up on her body." The caller was even more convinced now that his colleague was guilty of murder.

When the caller broached the possibility of DNA testing, I made my move. "Can you get me Moss's DNA? Can you send me a glass he drank from or, better yet, some strands of hair?" He wasn't sure. "I felt it was my duty to tell you what's going on," he said. "I don't know about stealing the guy's DNA."

"Look, there's strong reason to believe he killed my aunt. But we can't bring him to justice if we don't have solid proof. His DNA would provide that proof," I pleaded. After more coaxing, he finally agreed. I passed on some tips Jim Starrs had given me about the handling of DNA evidence. "Place the evidence in a paper bag, not a plastic one," I said. "Condensation that builds up in a plastic bag could contaminate the evidence."

"I'll try, but the guy's meticulous. When he has a drink, he washes the glass out, like, two seconds later. The same thing with food. He usually eats everything in front of him, but when he doesn't, he sticks the leftovers in the bottom of the trash bag and takes the trash out."

I told the caller to do his best. "Wait for the opportunity; don't try to force anything," I advised.

The caller's opportunity came quickly. He found a beer glass Moss had been drinking from, wrapped it in a brown paper bag, and sent it off to Professor Starrs.

Two weeks later, Starrs called me in the newsroom with the results. "I'm truly sorry, but there's about twenty different DNA profiles on this beer mug. It's got to be the dirtiest glass I've ever seen," he chuckled. "Ask your man in New Hampshire to get me a hair sample. And tell him to get a new dishwasher for the bar."

While the caller was waiting for another opportunity to get a sample of Moss's DNA for testing, I set out to find Mary's roommates. Pat Delmore and Pam Parker had never shared their story with anyone. Both women were from Massachusetts, but they seemed to have vanished after Mary's murder. I sought help from my colleagues on the WBZ I-Team, giving them the names of Mary's roommates as well as the name of Nathan Ward, Mary's former boyfriend. I didn't think he had killed Mary, but it seemed worth talking with him. Their volatile relationship still disturbed me, although the evidence against Moss and his recent behavior made him a much stronger suspect in my eyes.

The I-Team found out that Nathan Ward had died of a heart attack in the Seattle area in the early 1990s. They also tracked down a Patricia Delmore who was living in Florida. When I called the Florida number, the man who answered told me I had the right Pat Delmore but the wrong state. She now was living in California. I located a number for Delmore in Santa Barbara. When I got her on the phone, she told me she was paying close attention to our reinvestigation. She said, "For years, I thought it

was Albert DeSalvo, but you've certainly made me re-
think that. Poor Mary, it was such a horrible time. It was
something I couldn't talk about for years. She was such a
sweet girl. I had met her in the Filene's cafeteria. She had
a sad look on her face. When I asked her what was wrong,
Mary told me that she needed a place to stay in Boston or
she'd have to move back home to Cape Cod. Of course,
I told her she could stay with Pam and me. It would be
crowded, but it would be fun. I now wish that Mary had
said no. We never went back to that apartment. This has
affected me for years. I have a daughter, and when she
told me that she was moving in with two girls, I almost
cried, I was so scared about what could happen to her."

Pat Delmore had a lot to get off her chest, so I just let
her talk. But eventually I turned the conversation toward
Preston Moss. "What was he like?" I asked.

"He was a very sharp dresser and acted like a perfect
gentleman with me. My sister, however, thought he was
kind of strange."

I asked Pat if Moss could have been capable of murder. "Oh, God, I hope not," she replied.

Delmore also told me she had not spoken to Pam
Parker in ten years, and I was having no luck finding her
on my own, but around that time, I did locate a relative of
another strangler victim. Major Tim Palmbach of the
Connecticut State Police, a Starrs team member, gave a
speech on forensic science in New Haven during which
he mentioned the Mary Sullivan case. Palmbach had attended Mary's exhumation and had worked with the
famed forensic scientist Dr. Henry Lee on some of the tis-
sue samples. Following the speech, an African American
man in his mid-sixties approached Palmbach. "Is it true?"
he asked. "Can you find the man who really murdered

Mary Sullivan?" Palmbach said it was a distinct possibility. The man began weeping. "Sophie Clark was my cousin," he told Palmbach. "She, too, was killed in the Boston Strangler case, and our family never believed it was Albert DeSalvo."

Palmbach put me in touch with the man. "I was Sophie's only relative living in Boston," he told me. "I promised her parents that I would look out for her. It was me who had to identify her body and bring her back to New Jersey for burial."

"I'll help you find her killer if you come forward and help us," I pledged.

Sophie Clark's cousin was in a difficult position, as it turned out. He knew that authorities had lied by claiming DeSalvo was the Boston Strangler, but he was now a member of the law enforcement establishment himself. "Sophie's family to me, but so are my brother cops. I just can't go public right now," he said. "I will say good luck and I'll be watching."

So here was another relative telling me how much he appreciated our work but that he wanted no part of it. Who could blame him? And if relatives of the victims were reluctant to join me, I doubted that family members of those who had perpetrated the great charade of a guilty DeSalvo would be willing to help, either. Still, I had to push on. Reading over John Bottomly's obituary, I noticed he had moved his family out west after his legal career had ended in scandal in Massachusetts. I knew that DeSalvo's original confession tapes had never been turned over to the state. Did his children have the tapes? What else might they have? If there was a deal to deliver DeSalvo to the public as the Boston Strangler, perhaps Bottomly had kept a record of it. I tracked down a Utah telephone number for his daughter, Holly Bottomly. I called her and explained our battle against the Massachusetts attorney general's office. At first, she sounded unfriendly, probably offended at the idea that her father had not caught the Boston Strangler. I could see I was using the wrong approach. Quickly switching gears, I said, "Holly, your dad may have been an honest man, but he was duped by those around him who looked to profit off the case. Do you think your father would not like to finally set things straight?" Of course, I said this believing that her father was one of the masterminds behind DeSalvo's false confession.

Bottomly broke down on the phone. She told me the family had kept all of her father's documents from the Boston Strangler case. "What about the confession tapes?" I asked. "We have everything!" she replied. We continued to talk over the next several days. We were getting along so well that I figured it was only a matter of time before I booked a flight to Salt Lake City to retrieve the evidence. But then our conversations took a different turn. She began to ask for money. Money for her mother, money for her, and money for the other Bottomly children. With a new baby, I couldn't afford to pay the Bottomly family, but Elaine and Dan Sharp offered to buy everything the family had kept from their father's past. A deal was about to be made when suddenly Holly Bottomly no longer wanted money or anything to do with our case. "I've been told not to cooperate with you," she said. She wouldn't give us a name but said that a friend of her father's had demanded that she stay away from us. What forces were working behind the scenes to keep us from the truth?

In July 2001, Reilly publicly challenged our motive

for getting involved in the case and our commitment to it, telling reporters that Richard DeSalvo had refused to give a sample of his DNA to be used in the attorney general's investigation. What Reilly didn't tell the media was that DeSalvo had offered his blood to the state many times over the preceding two years on the condition that independent scientists test the evidence. Richard did not trust the government, and after reading Gerry Leone's affidavit, I could hardly blame him.

News of Reilly's latest chess move infuriated Elaine Sharp. "Why do you have to rule out a dead guy in order to go after a living suspect?" she asked reporters. Sharp was referring to my previous statements to the press about a suspect in Mary's murder, whom I did not name, living in northern New England. "Fine. They want Richard's DNA, we'll give it to them. In public!" she swore.

This set the stage for a public bloodletting. Elaine Sharp called in a physician friend of hers to take DeSalvo's blood and saliva before the cameras on July 18, 2001. At first, I opposed the idea of a staged event, and Richard appeared embarrassed by it. "It doesn't matter what the press writes," Elaine promised. "People will see Richard giving his DNA, and that will put the ball back squarely in Reilly's court." Reporters from all the local television stations and newspapers came to cover the event. The cameras clicked away as Dr. Stephen Miller pricked Richard's finger and ran a cotton swab along the roof of his mouth. I could sense the disdain coming from members of the media. We had worked very hard to get the public on our side, and I hoped we were doing the right thing. A stoic figure in short sleeves, Richard turned in the direction of the gang of reporters, but he could not see them. Blindness had robbed Richard of his eyesight, but it did not rob him of his pride. He looked uneasy and I could tell he hated every minute in the spotlight. "I honestly swear on a stack of Bibles that Al wasn't the Boston Strangler," he told reporters. "If I ever thought he even killed one, I wouldn't be sitting here today."

As our media event made clear, we were fully ready to swap evidence, but the attorney general wasn't. Tom Reilly's office released a statement that day saying, "It is critical that it [the investigation] be conducted impartially and that the integrity of the evidence be preserved."

Most press reports treated the exercise fairly, but Reilly had his supporters, especially the *Boston Globe* columnist Brian McGrory. McGrory had been given a major scoop when Reilly told him and only him that his office had reopened Mary's murder case. This was payback time. In a column titled "Not the Way to Help Out," McGrory wrote, "Enough already. That stunt pulled by Richard DeSalvo last week when he called a news conference and sought to barter his freshly drawn blood to the state Attorney General was at once shameless and shameful. . . . What Reilly seems to want is a by-the-books investigation, and so far, so good. What Sherman and DeSalvo seem to want is a circus, with hokey press conferences and televised exhumations." What McGrory didn't mention was that the state could afford to fight our lawsuit and bury us under a blizzard of paperwork. If we as families couldn't get authorities to do their jobs, at least we could utilize our biggest strength, media coverage, to change public opinion.

But not everyone on our side agreed with this assessment. For the first time, my mother voiced her strong disapproval about the direction in which the case was heading. "Mary was a dignified girl," she told me. "These public displays only make a mockery of her life—and her death. Show the world the real evidence, Case; you don't have to resort to this." It had been nearly a year since Mary's exhumation, and we still had no idea about the results of the forensic work being conducted by Jim Starrs and his team. Sharp had flown down to Washington on several occasions to see if Starrs had found any trace of Mary's killer on her remains, but the professor told her his team was still months away from releasing its findings. I worried that Starrs was merely putting off the bad news that the forensic investigation had been a colossal waste of time.

I began having doubts about Starrs's work at the same time that Richard DeSalvo was making the painful decision to have his brother's body exhumed. Richard held out hope that if Starrs had found evidence of Mary's killer on her body, it would be possible to find evidence of Albert's killer on his remains. The attack on Albert DeSalvo had been carried out at close quarters, so it was conceivable that the murderer's blood, hair, or saliva had passed onto the victim's skin.

In October 2001, a full year after Mary's exhumation, Starrs's team and members of the DeSalvo family gathered at Puritan Lawn Cemetery in Peabody to watch as Albert's casket was hoisted out of the dirt. The team worked fast, and the exhumation took less than an hour. Starrs did not inspect the remains at the grave site; instead, DeSalvo's casket was placed in the back of a hearse and driven to a laboratory in York, Pennsylvania.

Unlike Mary's exhumation, this one was done under a veil of secrecy. Starrs feared that if Tom Reilly found out about it, he might claim that the professor was tampering with evidence and post state troopers at the Massachusetts border to arrest Starrs and his team.

At the Pennsylvania laboratory, the forensic team received quite a shock when they opened the casket. Albert DeSalvo's heart, lungs, and kidneys were missing. Starrs already knew that the vital organs had been taken out during the 1973 autopsy, but he was startled to find that they had not been put back, as is standard procedure after an autopsy. The Sharps did not believe they had simply been misplaced. "It's frightening to think that DeSalvo's organs might be in a collector's jar somewhere," Dan said. We already knew that authorities had taken certain pieces of evidence as trophies in the case, but the idea that someone had stolen DeSalvo's vital organs was not just disturbing but macabre. The news also did not bode well for Tom Reilly. He had staunchly defended the state's refusal to share evidence with the families because he was concerned about chain of custody issues. Yet someone working on behalf of the state had stolen DeSalvo's organs. Who could better be trusted with the evidence—the families who only wanted justice, or the state of Massachusetts?

21 : Truth or Consequences

Waking early on the morning of December 5, 2001, I tossed and turned while my wife tried unsuccessfully to cuddle me in her arms. My mind was solely on Mary's murder and whether Albert DeSalvo had been her killer. It was a question I had wrestled with for ten years, my mother for much longer. In twenty-four hours, Jim Starrs and his forensic team would announce their findings to the world. I would be flying down to Washington with Elaine and Dan Sharp. My mother had decided to stay on Cape Cod. She wanted the opportunity to pray at Mary's graveside when she heard the news.

Before leaving the house, I shared a quiet moment with Laura and our baby daughter. "You did the right thing, honey, no matter what the outcome is. Your mom will finally know," my wife told me. I hugged her tightly. She had been my backbone. Walking out the door, I wondered, "Will I return home a hero or a fool?" When I met the Sharps for the ride to the airport, I suspected they were thinking the same thing. The Sharps had taken our case on faith and had worked long and hard to defend the view that DeSalvo was innocent. The evidence we had gathered pointed away from Albert DeSalvo, but our theories would be blown apart if DNA put him at the scene of the crime. My credibility as a journalist was at stake, too, but that was nothing compared to what my mother and Richard DeSalvo were going through. Mom's relationship with her siblings, who wanted to keep the past dead and buried, had nearly been destroyed by her vow to find Mary's killer. Richard had given up a quiet life to endure intense public scrutiny. Yet both had had the courage to see this investigation through to the end, whatever the end might be.

On the eve of the announcement, while driving back to our hotel from dinner, Dan told a story that calmed my growing anxiety. "A few years ago," he began. "I took a case of a mentally retarded man who was severely beaten while living in state care. His name was Joey. He was in his fifties and had been in state facilities his whole life. He even had a retarded brother whom he hadn't seen in years because the brother had simply vanished in the system. Can you believe the state of Massachusetts lost his brother?" Dan asked, still outraged. "Joey was beaten by another disabled person living at the same halfway house. This guy had abused other residents as well. There was little supervision at the house, so you can see how easily an attack like this could happen. I sued the state to make sure that Joey was taken care of for the rest of his life. The state fought tooth and nail, but the jury sided with Joey. They awarded him millions. I didn't care about the money; I just wanted someone held responsible so it wouldn't happen again. Joey didn't care about the money, either. He just wanted a new radio for his tiny bedroom.

But when the jury decision came down, it was the most satisfying moment of my legal career. We had really done something good. I guess what I'm trying to say, Casey, is that I feel the same way about this case. We've really done some good."

Dan's story eased my mind, and that night, I slept soundly for the first time in days.

The scientific findings in the Mary Sullivan murder case were announced the next day, December 6, 2001, at the National Press Club in Washington. By the time we arrived, the room was filled to capacity with journalists from all over the world. Fortunately, Starrs had reserved three seats for us in the front row. Seated on the platform in front of a large blue and yellow George Washington University banner were Starrs, Baden, Dr. Bruce Goldberger from the University of Florida, and David Foran, head of the molecular biology lab at George Washington University. Standing up and walking behind the lectern, Starrs welcomed members of the media and then he recited the problems he and his team had faced in Boston. "Any relationship we might have had with Massachusetts authorities who are in possession of a number of items in this case, all of that cooperation that scientists would love to have in the open air of free discussion, we have been deprived of," he told the reporters. "Massachusetts authorities have stonewalled us from the outset.

"The question we set out to answer today was, Did Albert DeSalvo rape and murder Mary Sullivan?" Starrs continued. A picture of Mary's smiling face was projected onto a large screen behind him. He spoke briefly about the difficult task of exhuming Mary's body and the fact that even her death certificate had contained a basic factual error. "The death certificate had her buried at Oak

Neck Cemetery in Hyannis, when we know she was buried at St. Francis Xavier Cemetery in Centerville, Massachusetts," he pointed out. After providing a brief background of Mary's murder, Starrs surrendered the microphone to Dr. Michael Baden, who had conducted the new autopsy.

Baden, a bear of a man, eased his way to the lectern. "The first question medical examiners ask is, How will the body look?" he said. "The remains were in fair condition, some in excellent condition. The body showed deterioration of the extremities, but the chest, abdomen, and pelvis were in excellent condition." Baden then began to dissect DeSalvo's confession as expertly as he would a human body. "DeSalvo said he entered Mary Sullivan's apartment at 4:00 P.M. and left when it was dark. But when the medical examiner arrived at the scene, he noticed that rigor mortis was complete." Baden pointed out that it takes several hours for the body to become fully rigid. "The time of death would have to have been many hours before 4:00 P.M.," he noted. Baden also had discovered that the medical examiner's inspection of Mary's stomach found only brown fluid, which smelled like coffee. Mary had yet to eat anything that day. It was inconceivable that Mary could go a full day without at least a snack of some kind. "So again, Sullivan was killed around ten o'clock in the morning, not four or four-thirty," Baden surmised.

Now the picture of Mary's smiling face was replaced on the overhead screen by an X ray of her skull. "Albert DeSalvo said he beat her unconscious and bit her over her body," Baden said, but there was no indication of blunt trauma to Mary's skull or bite marks on her skin.

The projectionist advanced slides from the skull X ray

to a picture of Mary's hyoid bone. Baden said, "The hyoid bone is a horseshoe-shaped bone right above the Adam's apple. It's the bone that the tongue is fixed to. It's the target organ for manual strangulation. Albert DeSalvo claimed that he manually strangled Sullivan with his thumbs against her Adam's apple." Baden noted that the hyoid bone is likely to fracture under the pressure of manual strangulation. "But as you can see," he pointed out, "Sullivan's hyoid bone shows absolutely no sign of trauma." I glanced over at Elaine, who was now smiling. As comfortable in a laboratory as in a courtroom, she had been the first person to raise the issue of the hyoid bone with Starrs and Baden. I then turned to watch the flurry of activity behind me. Reporters were scribbling on notepads, summarizing Baden's presentation. What it boiled down to was that Albert DeSalvo had lied when he confessed to the murder of Mary Sullivan.

The next presenter was Dr. Bruce Goldberger, the team's toxicology expert. Starrs wanted the world to know that he had all the bases covered. Goldberger's tests detected neither drugs nor alcohol in Mary's body.

The fourth speaker was the team's DNA expert, David Foran. Jim Starrs, who clearly knew how to put on a show, had saved the best for last. The slender Foran fidgeted at the podium. "This has been a huge amount of work," he observed. "This was completely uncharted territory. We had to pick out evidence we thought would be most productive." First, Foran and his DNA team had looked at Mary's fingernails, he said. "If she fought off her attacker, she could have scratched him. But the only DNA found under Sullivan's fingernails was her own," he added. As Foran continued, my hopes for a clear conclusion began to fade. Foran had also examined Mary's

underwear, which had been put on her right before the funeral. "We were looking for any possible leakage [from
the vagina]," he explained. Foran indicated that under ultraviolet light, he had discovered fluorescents in the
panties, an indication of the presence of biological fluids.
The DNA sequence found on the panties did not match
Mary Sullivan or Albert DeSalvo, but it could have come
from the medical examiner or even the mortician. Foran
also had discovered something in Mary's pubic hair. "The
substance was clear and crusted," he said. "It was not
brittle." In short, it had the characteristics of semen. I sat
up in my chair. Mary's murder had been a sex crime, and
this was the killer's DNA, plain and simple. Did DeSalvo
do it? David Foran was about to tell the world. "These genetic sequences did not match Mary Sullivan," he said.
"They did not match anyone on the forensic team, and
most important, the DNA is not from Albert DeSalvo."

The reporters let out a collective gasp. A wave of emotion came crashing over me. We were right. Albert De-
Salvo had not killed Mary. Through our hard work
history was being rewritten. Now David Foran took his
seat, and Jim Starrs returned to the podium. "The family
of Mary Sullivan, Casey Sherman and Diane Dodd, and
their determination to seek the truth over many years
have been vindicated," he said. "We have found evidence, and it does not and cannot be associated with Albert DeSalvo."

Starrs then called me to the podium. I said, "I started
to look at this case ten years ago because of what my
mother said to me, which was, 'I don't believe Albert De-
Salvo killed Mary, and I believe her killer . . . is still out
there.'" I had to stop. My voice was breaking. I took off
my glasses and wiped my eyes. "We were just looking for

one thing," I continued, "which was the answer to the question Did he do it? Now we have the answer, and what we've heard today brings my mother a certain closure in this case. It also gives the DeSalvo family closure to this case. Because if Albert DeSalvo didn't kill my aunt, which he confessed to, then he probably didn't kill any of those women." DNA evidence had proved that DeSalvo had not murdered my aunt, and I believed that his grossly inaccurate confessions to the ten other murders proved he had not been the Boston Strangler after all. "The real killers are still out there, and we need to bring them to justice," I concluded.

As I stepped off the podium, reporters quickly swarmed around me. But before I could talk to them, I had to talk to someone else. Elaine Sharp hugged me and handed me her cell phone, saying, "Call your mom." Reaching her at home, I found out she had already heard the news. David Foran had called her right before the press conference. As we spoke, she began to cry. "You did it, Case!" she said. "It's all because of you. Thank you so much." I had waited ten years to hear those words. "No, you did it Mom," I replied. I looked in the direction of Elaine, Dan, and Jim Starrs. "We all did it!"

22 : The Final Showdown

"So what are you going to do now?" Jim Mellon asked as we both watched a seagull fly overhead with what looked to be a small fish in its mouth. It was a beautiful sight, even though many New Englanders feel that seagulls are merely rodents with wings.

I said, "I think the world now knows that DeSalvo wasn't the Boston Strangler. The only person who doesn't seem to know it is Tom Reilly." A strong wind was blowing off the ocean. I zipped up my coat and blew warm breath over my frozen hands. "I never set out to exonerate Albert DeSalvo. I'm glad it happened for his family because they've certainly been through enough. But my goal is to find Mary's killer, and I'm not going to stop until I do."

Mellon smiled. "You'll nail the bastard," he said. "I'd be a fool to bet against you."

I did not tell Mellon that my man in New Hampshire had finally succeeded in getting Preston Moss's DNA. One evening, Moss had left his baseball cap at the bar, and the man had taken the cap back into the storage room and with a pair of tweezers pulled out several strands of Moss's hair, placed them in a paper bag, and shipped the bag to David Foran's lab for testing. The tests showed that Moss's hair partially matched DNA evidence found on Mary's body. The evidence was promising, but it still did not scientifically prove he was the killer. The mitochondrial DNA test performed on the evidence could exclude Moss as the killer but could not incriminate him. The DNA test showed the odds are one in five that Moss murdered Mary. "We still have a long way to go," Elaine Sharp told me. "The hair sample was a good start, but we need Moss's blood to really prove he did it. If only the attorney general's office could force him to submit to a blood test," Sharp sighed. "That could answer the question once and for all." We both believed, however, that Tom Reilly was not interested in pursuing this case. We would have to do it on our own.

With the help of a private investigator friend, I also had tracked down Mary's missing roommate, Pamela Parker. "I don't think she wants to be found," he told me. "She has no credit cards in her name; everything was put in the husband's name. She may not want to speak with you, but good luck."

I dialed Parker's number, hoping she wouldn't slam the phone down the minute I told her who I was. Instead, Parker was relieved to hear my voice. "I've been trying to get in touch with you for the longest time," she said. "You have to understand. It was the worst time in my life. I never believed that DeSalvo was the killer, and you finally proved it."

I did not want to bait her with a list of possible suspects. Rather, I wanted her honest opinion. "Who do you think really murdered Mary?" I asked.

"Honestly, I think it was Pat's old boyfriend, Preston Moss," she replied. "I had a strange feeling that he hated your aunt, that he was jealous of her for some reason. Pat had been hanging out with Mary, and not spending much time with Preston. A group of us would all be sitting around that small apartment, singing songs, everyone in a happy and mellow mood. I remember glancing over at Preston, who was staring at your aunt. She was on the other side of the room, singing and laughing, oblivious to his stare. It wasn't a friendly stare. It looked like he detested her. It looked like he wanted to get up and choke her right there. It was very strange." Parker added that she had received a threatening phone call from a man who sounded like Moss shortly after Mary's murder. The caller warned that he would do to her what he had done to "that Mary bitch."

After hearing Pam Parker's story, I wondered why the attorney general's office had not spoken with her. Tom Reilly had also dismissed Jim Starrs's DNA findings out of hand, without ever examining the results. If Mary's murder case was open and active, then why wasn't the attorney general pursuing these leads? I thought I knew the answer. Tom Reilly wanted Albert DeSalvo to be the Boston Strangler. He did not want to dig into the dark past of the attorney general's office; his goal was to protect the institution. I believe that economics also played a role in Reilly's decision against pursuing this case. If the state granted that Albert DeSalvo had not killed Mary Sullivan, it would be forced to reopen the other ten Boston Strangler murders. The cost of such an undertaking would be in the tens of millions.

On December 24, 2001, Suffolk Superior Court Judge Guy Volterra dismissed our lawsuit against the state of

Massachusetts, in which we had sought to obtain evidence and personal items connected to the murder of Mary Sullivan. "So long as the criminal investigation remains ongoing and the items are required as evidence, the plaintiffs have no right to possess that evidence," Volterra ruled. Though I felt deflated by the decision, Dan Sharp reminded me, "We proved that Albert DeSalvo didn't kill Mary. No court can take that away from us."

A few months later, in March 2002, the Massachusetts Board of Bar Overseers announced that F. Lee Bailey had been banned from practicing law in the state. The ruling followed similar decisions by the state of Florida and the United States Supreme Court that were based on Bailey's mishandling of six million dollars' worth of stock belonging to a client convicted of drug smuggling. Bailey's disbarment was the first good news I'd heard since the DNA results. Meanwhile, I was wondering what to do next. There was little hope of holding Preston Moss accountable in a court of law. I did not believe authorities were serious about solving Mary's murder. I had promised my mother when this strange journey began that I would find Mary's killer, and Mom could not wait another thirty years for the truth.

I believed that the truth was waiting for me in New Hampshire. Before departing on my ride north, I wrote letters to my wife and young daughter, telling them that no matter what happened, I wanted them to know that I had tried to do the right thing. I also told my baby girl that one day she might be called on to stand up for what she believed in, and I explained to Laura and Isabella that their love had made my life complete. I put the letters away in a drawer and hoped they would never have to read them.

I did not know what to expect from a confrontation

with Preston Moss. But I knew that if he felt threatened, there was a chance he would attack me. In the summer, Moss worked as a golf instructor at a resort in the White Mountains. I called the resort and spoke directly to him. Disguising my voice, I scheduled a golf lesson under the name Wayne Rose. Fortunately, there had been a cancellation, and Moss penciled me in for an afternoon lesson.

The drive would take about three hours. I gassed up the Blazer and leafed through my collection of CDs. Santana was too mellow, Springsteen's latest offering too somber. I opened the cover to the *Eminem Show* and slid the disk into the CD player. Later, I pulled over to the side of the road, placed my daughter's car seat in the trunk, and peeled off the Elmo reflectors from the back windows. I also took off my wedding ring and put it in the glove compartment. I knew much about Preston Moss, but I did not want him to know a thing about me. I especially did not want him to know I had a family.

I cut a path through Boston and followed Interstate 93 north. It was late September, and the leaves had just begun to turn color. The farther north I drove, the more spectacular the scenery. As my Chevy chewed up the miles, I thought about what my mother and I had been through. I knew the final answer lay ahead of me.

The golf resort was right off the highway. I had never played golf in my life, but I sure did look the part of a golfer in my khaki shorts, golf shirt, baseball cap, and dark sunglasses. My man in New Hampshire had told me that Moss was paying very close attention to the Boston Strangler case and had seen me numerous times on television. I hoped my little disguise would work.

Pulling off at the exit, I took a quick drive around the town where the resort was located, a quaint little village sprinkled with roadside shops. Norman Rockwell could have set his easel up here and painted a fine picture of Americana. It was beautiful, but it eerily reminded me of Orson Welles's film *The Stranger,* in which Welles played a Nazi war criminal who tried to hide from his past by working as a teacher in a small New England town. Was Preston Moss also trying to hide from his past?

It was almost one o'clock when I pulled into the resort parking lot. The golf course was busy. The temperature was nearly eighty degrees and the sun shone brilliantly in the sky. I took a deep breath and made my way to the pro shop. On my way, I spotted a golf cart pulling up ahead of me, driven by a man who looked like Moss. I needed more time to prepare myself. I ducked into the pro shop and stayed behind a rack of clothes, pretending to compare prices on golf shirts, when suddenly I heard a voice behind me. "Are you Wayne Rose?" the man asked. Preston Moss was standing there. "Uh, yes, I am," I replied.

Until now, I had seen only pictures of the prime suspect in my aunt's murder. He appeared to be in his late fifties. His once bright red hair was now almost completely gray. Moss stood about five foot, eight inches. He did not look like a killer, but then, most Nazi war criminals looked like accountants.

To my relief, Moss did not recognize me. "Do you want to work on your short game or your long game?" he asked. I had no idea what he was talking about. "I'd like to work on my short game," I replied, hoping he wouldn't ask me any more questions. "Great, I'll get the cart and take you to your clubs," Moss said cheerfully. I followed him outside and watched him put a bag of balls in the golf cart. Then he drove the cart back in my direction and pulled up alongside me. "Hop in, Wayne!" he said with a smile. I took off my hat and dark sunglasses. "My name isn't Wayne Rose. It's Casey Sherman," I announced. Moss's smile turned to a look of fear. His eyes grew wide, and his hands began to tremble.

"I . . . I have nothing to say to you. You can talk to my lawyer," he shouted.

"Well, your lawyer's not here, and I need to ask you a few questions about Mary Sullivan," I replied, all traces of nervousness now gone. Preston Moss wasn't the bogeyman I had envisioned for so long. He was just a pathetic creature running away from his past.

"I said, talk to my lawyer!" he barked once again.

"I don't want to create a scene, Preston," I said calmly. "But if that's what you want, I'd be more than happy to."

Moss must have seen my point. He collected himself and began speaking in hushed tones. "I didn't do it," he insisted. "I remember going to your aunt's apartment the night before the murder and hearing a strange voice coming from inside. I never saw him."

"Yet you were able to describe him to police," I pointed out. The police had found Moss's statement untruthful, and it was one of the reasons they had begun to investigate him as a suspect.

"I . . . I don't remember. That was a long time ago."

"Tell me, what were you doing the day of the murder?" I asked.

"That I vividly remember. I slept in late, like most college kids do. Then I watched football on TV all day with my grandfather."

"Do you remember who was playing?"

"No, as I said, it was a long time ago."

"Yes, I guess you're right. Is there anyone who can vouch for your whereabouts that day?"

"My mother and grandfather, but they're both dead."

"So no one can corroborate your alibi?"

Moss shifted uneasily on the seat of the golf cart. "I didn't kill her! My mind was on my schoolwork. I had finals coming up. I studied all night and watched football the next day."

"Wait a minute. First you tell me that you visited Mary's apartment the night before the murder; now you say you were studying all night. Which is it, Preston?"

"Ah . . . talk . . . talk to my lawyer!" Moss responded, his stutter surfacing for the first time in our conversation.

"Listen," I told him, "we may have your DNA at the crime scene. We have witnesses; we have the lie detector tests. Here's what I think happened, Preston. You broke into the apartment to find evidence that your girlfriend was cheating on you, but instead, you found Mary moving her belongings in. She caught you rifling through Pat's letters and demanded answers. An argument ensued, and you turned violent and strangled her. What you did to her body afterwards, I cannot understand. You are an evil man. I promised to find Mary's killer, and I may have, regardless of the fact that you'll probably never be prosecuted. I know you did it."

Moss pleaded his innocence once again, and in a strange move, he extended his hand to me. I slapped it away, then turned and walked back to my car.

While I drove home, I concluded iron bars were not needed to jail Mary's killer. If Moss did it, then he was already in a psychological prison. He was being guarded twenty-four hours a day by a conscience that would not let him forget what he had done.

It was now late afternoon, and the hazy orange skyline

of Boston was just ahead of me. Normally, I would drive right through the city to the Southeast Expressway and home. But on this day, I made my way back to Charles Street, back to where it had all begun. Double-parking my Blazer on the one-way street, I stopped briefly at a flower shop. Then, walking the two blocks to 44A, I glanced up at my aunt's apartment building and whispered a prayer.

"You can rest now," I said softly. I leaned down and placed a single rose on the front step. It was a rose for Mary.

A few days later, still bothered by Moss's alibi, I asked a colleague at WBZ to assist me in some research. Moss claimed he had been watching football on television the day of Mary's murder. Could this be true? After leafing through a couple of thick sports encyclopedias, we found our answer. No college or professional football games were played or televised on January 4, 1964.

Epilogue

In October 2002, I called the attorney general's office to offer investigators the evidence I had gathered against the prime suspect in my aunt's murder. Gerry Leone having left the attorney general's office to spearhead the state's counterterrorism task force, I scheduled a meeting with his replacement, Kurt Schwartz. "I'm writing a book on the case," I told him on the telephone. "If you're serious about finding Mary's killer, you'll want to hear what we've uncovered."

On the day of the meeting, I waited in the reception area for more than an hour. Schwartz never showed up; his secretary said he had had to attend a meeting in western Massachusetts. I received a phone call from him later that day. At first, I thought he was calling to apologize for missing our meeting, but I was wrong.

"I'm canceling the meeting," he said.

"Kurt, I have found the prime suspect. If you still consider her murder an open and active investigation, you have to meet with me."

"There will be no meeting, and that is final," he stated.

The Massachusetts attorney general's office is trying to keep the Mary Sullivan case dead and buried. However, I will continue to compile evidence against the killer, for my mother and for Mary. When I began my investigation, I hoped to find the real Boston Strangler, but the Boston Strangler was a myth. Jack the Ripper had not been resurrected to stalk the women of Boston. In my search for one killer, I instead discovered there were many. George Nassar should be questioned in the killings of Nina Nichols, Ida Irga, and Jane Sullivan. Nassar may have also been the brown-haired man witnesses described in connection with the Evelyn Corbin murder. Other victims may have had other killers. Jim Mellon believes that one victim was murdered by her own son, and there is enough evidence to suspect Patricia Bissette's lover and boss in her death. Sophie Clark's killer was most likely a black man seen leaving her building the day of the murder, a man who later failed two lie detector tests in connection with the crime. Anna Slesers and Helen Blake may have been strangled by a housepainter. The fact that the painter was working outside the buildings of both women on the day they were killed is certainly suspicious. Finally, Beverly Samans's killer may have been one of her mentally challenged students from the Fernald School. Daniel Pennachio's confession to that crime was more accurate than was Albert DeSalvo's. Until these murders are truly solved, the Boston Strangler case will haunt New England.

Author's Note

All the characters in this book are real, but I have used pseudonyms for a few of them to protect their privacy. However, be assured that the Massachusetts attorney general's office does know the real name of the prime suspect in my aunt's murder. In recreating dialogue from the original strangler investigation, I have relied on the most credible witnesses to the events and the documents that I believe contain the most accurate accounts. Always my intention has been to remain faithful to the people written about in this book, and to the events as they really happened.

Bibliography

LAW ENFORCEMENT AGENCY REPORTS

Death Certificate for Patricia Bissette. City of Boston. January 3, 1963.

Patricia Bissette Autopsy Report. Case No. LME 9105.

Report on Scene Examination, Clothing, RE: Homicide Patricia Bissette. Case #220. By Deputy Supt. John J. Slattery Jr., Boston Police Department. January 9, 1963.

Analysis of Statements Made by Albert DeSalvo. Case 08: Patricia Bissette.

Helen E. Blake Autopsy Report. Case 62-179.

Analysis of Statements Made by Albert DeSalvo. Case 03: Helen Blake.

Mary E. Brown Autopsy Report. Case 63-57.

Examination of Material in connection with the Death of Mary E. Brown. By Arthur McBay. March 21, 1963.

Postmortem Examination on the Body of Mary E. Brown. Case 63-57.

Death Record of Mary Brown. City of Lawrence. March 16, 1966.

Analysis of Statements Made by Albert DeSalvo. Case 13: Mary Brown.

Report on Scene: Examination Homicide 315 Huntington Avenue. Sophie Clark. By Deputy-Supt. Arthur Cadegan Jr., Boston Police Department. December 6, 1962.

Death Record of Sophie Clark. City of Boston. December 11, 1962.

Interrogation of Albert DeSalvo in regard to Sophie Clark. Transcripts of tapes.

Analysis of Statements Made by Albert DeSalvo. Case 07: Sophie Clark.

Further investigation of Albert DeSalvo (Background Information re: Case 07—Sophie Clark). From Andrew Tuney and Phillip DiNatale to John Bottomly. December 8, 1965.

Further investigation of Albert DeSalvo in regard to Case 07: Sophie Clark. From Andrew Tuney and Phillip DiNatale to John Bottomly. February 15, 1966.

Evelyn Corbin Autopsy Report. Case 63-243. By J. Robert Shaughnessy, M.D. September 25, 1963.

Postmortem Examination of the Body of Evelyn Corbin. Case: 63-243.

Death Record of Evelyn Corbin. City of Salem. March 16, 1966.

Analysis of Statements Made by Albert H. DeSalvo. Case 09: Evelyn Corbin.

Examination of Materials in connection with the Fatal Strangulation of Joann Graff. By Arthur McBay. December 10, 1963.

Joann Graff Autopsy Report. Case 63-327.

Death Record of Joann M. Graff. City of Lawrence. March 16, 1966.

Analysis of Statements Made by Albert DeSalvo. Case 10: Joann Graff.

Ida Irga Autopsy Report. From Dr. Michael Luongo to the district attorney of Suffolk County. August 21, 1962.

Examination of Materials in connection with the Fatal Strangulation of Ida Irga. By Arthur McBay, Chemical Laboratory, Massachusetts State Police. August 27, 1962.

Further Investigation of Albert DeSalvo—Information in regard to Case 06: Ida Irga. From Andrew Tuney to John Bottomly. January 26, 1966.

Interrogation of Albert DeSalvo in regard to Ida Irga. Transcripts of tapes.

Analysis of Statements Made by Albert DeSalvo. Case 02: Nina Nichols.

Examination of Materials in connection with the Deaths of Nina Nichols, Anna Slesers, and Jane Sullivan. By Arthur McBay, Chemical Laboratory, Massachusetts State Police. November 7, 1962.

Analysis of Statements Made by Albert DeSalvo. Case 01: Anna Slesers.

Further Investigation of Albert DeSalvo and Statements Made by Him in regard to Case 01: Anna Slesers. From Andrew Tuney and Phillip DiNatale to John Bottomly. October 1, 1965.

Medical Examiner's Report of View and Autopsy in the Case of Jane Sullivan. August 31, 1962.

Preliminary Report on Examination of Homicide Scene—Case #146—Jane Sullivan. August 31, 1962.

Supplementary Report on Examinations regarding the Homicide of Jane Sullivan. By C. Dana Kuhn, assistant biological chemist, Boston Police Department. September 3, 1962.

Death Record of Jane Sullivan. City of Boston. September 12, 1962.

Analysis of Statements Made by Albert DeSalvo. Case 06: Jane Sullivan.

Mary Anne Sullivan Autopsy Report. From Dr. Michael A. Luongo to the district attorney for Suffolk County. January 4, 1964.

Death Record of Mary Sullivan. City of Boston. January 10, 1964.

Analysis of Statements Made by Albert DeSalvo. Case 11: Mary Sullivan.

Further Investigation of Albert DeSalvo in regard to Case 11: Mary A. Sullivan. From Andrew Tuney and Phillip DiNatale to John Bottomly. February 7, 1966.

Interrogation of A. DeSalvo at MCI Bridgewater on March 6, 1965. Bailey tape.

Albert DeSalvo—General Suspect. From Officer Stephen C. Delaney to John Bottomly. March 11, 1965.

Crime Conditions—Boston. Re: Strangler. From special agent in charge, Boston, to director, FBI. September 20, 1965 (Freedom of Information Act. File Number: 163-12664).

Re: Albert Henry DeSalvo. From John Bottomly to James L. Handley, special agent in charge, FBI. October 29, 1965 (Freedom of Information Act. File Number: 163-12664).

Further investigation of Albert DeSalvo. From Andrew Tuney and Phillip DiNatale to John Bottomly. December 7, 1965.

Strangler Investigation Confidential Memorandum. From Herbert Travers to Edward Brooke. April 14, 1966.

United States Government Memorandum re: Albert H. DeSalvo. From W. V. Cleveland to Mr. Gale. UFAC-RAPE. February 25, 1967 (Freedom of Information Act. File Number: 163-12664).

BOOKS
Bailey, F. Lee, and Harvey Aronson. *The Defense Never Rests.* New York: Stein and Day, 1971.

Carroll, Bob, Michael Gershman, David Neft, and John Thorn. *Total Football*. New York: HarperCollins, 1997.

Frank, Gerold. *The Boston Strangler*. New York: Penguin Books, 1967.

Kelly, Susan. *The Boston Stranglers*. New York: Kensington Publishing, 1995.

Longley, Jennifer. *Images of America: Hyannis and Hyannis Port*. Charleston, S.C.: Arcadia Publishing, 2002.

Sheedy, Jack, and Jim Coogan. *Cape Cod Companion: The History and Mystery of Old Cape Cod*. East Dennis, Mass.: Harvest Home Books, 1999.

MAGAZINE ARTICLES

Byers, Margery. "Fear Walks Alone." *Life,* February 15, 1963.

Cavendish, Marshall. *Murder Casebook Volume 5: The Boston Strangler* (a Marshall Cavendish monthly publication), June 1985.

Kirkpatrick, Sidney. "The Psychic, the Shoe Salesman, and the Boston Strangler." *Los Angeles Times Magazine,* May 12, 2002.

NEWSPAPER AND WIRE SERVICE ARTICLES

"Another First for Brooke: Courthouse Bears His Name." *Boston Globe,* June 21, 2000.

"Attorney F. Lee Bailey Still Flying High." *Boston Globe,* May 15, 1988.

"Attorney Says DeSalvo Fears He'll Be Slain." United Press International, February 26, 1967.

"Bailey Disbarred by State." *Boston Globe,* March 23, 2002.

"Bailey Gets Jury Trial in Calif. Driving Case." Associated Press, March 16, 1982.

"Bailey Plays Perry Mason in Case of 'Boston Strangler.' " *Washington Post*, February 26, 1967.

"Bailey Takes Stand in Own Defense." *Boston Globe*, October 27, 1999.

"Bailey's Cross-Examination of Fuhrman Is Recalled." Associated Press, September 10, 1995.

"Boston Strangler Gives Up in Store." *Washington Post*, February 25, 1967.

"Boston Strangler Nephew Charged." *Boston Herald*, March 27, 1995.

"Bridgewater Makes Gains, but Flaws Remain." *Boston Globe*, March 13, 1989.

"Brooke Urges Reward Hike for Strangler." United Press International, January 17, 1964.

"Centerpiece/Thomas Troy for the Defense." *Boston Globe*, October 13, 1982.

"Court Eases 22-Year Ban on 'Titicut Follies.' " *Boston Globe*, September 29, 1989.

"Fighting Fire with . . . Change." *Boston Globe*, February 26, 2002.

"Flight of 'Strangler' Provides Rip-Roaring Story While It Lasts." *Washington Post*, February 26, 1967.

"Former Mass. Official Guilty of State Tax Evasion in 1973." *Boston Globe*, July 7, 1981.

"Hearst Seeks to Clear Record." Associated Press, March 6, 1980.

"Hearst to Get New Hearing." Associated Press, October 21, 1980.

"Hyannis Girl Strangled in Boston." *Cape Cod Standard Times*, January 5, 1964.

"Mad Strangler Doubted in Hyannis Girl's Case." United Press International, August 19, 1964.

"Major Crackdown on Mass. Tax Delinquents." *Boston Globe,* March 16, 1983.

McGrory, Brian. "Not a Way to Help Out." *Boston Globe,* July 24, 2001.

"Obituary: John S. Bottomly, at 63." *Boston Globe,* August 21, 1984.

"Obituary: Adolph Maffie." *Boston Globe,* September 28, 1988.

"Obituary: Edmund L. McNamara." *Boston Herald,* February 22, 2000.

"Obituary: Thomas Troy at 70." *Boston Globe,* February 15, 2000.

"Path of Juvenile Justice Is Explored." *Boston Globe,* January 24, 1982.

"Reilly Says He's Inclined to Offer Families Access to Boston Strangler Files." *Boston Globe,* May 12, 2000.

Wilson, Theo. "Bailey: 'Strangler' Is a Wild Vegetable." News Syndicate Co., February 27, 1967.

———. "The Real Issue at the Trial: Defendant DeSalvo's Mind." News Syndicate Co., January 18, 1967.

DOCUMENTARY FILM

History through the Lens. The Boston Strangler: A Legacy of Terror. Van Ness Films, Prometheus Entertainment, 2001.

Index

Quincy (Mass.), 130, 131
Raymond's Department Store
    (Boston), 174
*Record American. See Boston
    Record American*
Reilly, Tom, 135; access to
    case files denied by, 169,
    181; and Richard
    DeSalvo's DNA, 205–6;
    reinvestigation
    stonewalled by, 149, 176,
    217–18; Sharp and, 154;
    Starrs's DNA findings
    dismissed by, 219; and
    Strangler evidence,
    190–91, 193
Republican Party, 40
Rhode Island, 55
Richlin, Dean, 195
Robey, Ames, 57; and Boston
    Strangler profile, 59–60,
    112–13; on Bridgewater
    conditions, 56; as
    DeSalvo's confidant, 102;
    on DeSalvo's exhumation,
    137; on DeSalvo's
    familiarity with crime
    scenes, 76; on DeSalvo's
    memory, 70
Rothman, Jules, 32–33, 227
Rowe, Kenneth, 38
Royal Sonesta Hotel
    (Cambridge, Mass.), news
    conference at, 181
Russell, Laura. *See* Sherman,
    Laura (née Russell)

St. Anthony's Shrine
    (Boston), 17–18
St. Francis Xavier Cemetery
    (Hyannis, Mass.), 177, 185
St. Francis Xavier Church
    (Hyannis, Mass.), 13, 15,
    116
Salem (Mass.), 35–36
Samans, Beverly, murder of,
    33–35, 83, 173, 227
San Francisco, 106
Scheck, Barry, 118
Schwartz, Kurt, 226
Sea Street Beach (Hyannis,
    Mass.), 14, 85–86, 187
Senior Citizens Center
    (Hyannis, Mass.), 159–60
Setterlund, Stanley, 91
Shapiro, Robert, 107
Sharp, Dan, 155, 191–92,
    211, 220. *See also*
    Whitfield, Sharp & Sharp
    (law firm)
Sharp, Elaine Whitfield:
    character of, 155–56; and
    Richard DeSalvo's DNA,
    206–7; Eldredge and, 161;
    and hyoid bone, 214; and
    Moss, 199–200, 219; and
    Nassar, 170–71; at news
    conferences, 167–68, 180;
    and Sullivan
    exhumation/forensic
    reinvestigation, 186,
    207–8. *See also* Whitfield,
    Sharp & Sharp (law firm)
Sheppard, Sam, 61